SIR JOHN SOANE'S MUSEUM

PIRANESI, PAESTUM & SOANE

John Wilton-Ely

æ

SJSM

Published in the United Kingdom
by Azimuth Editions

Azimuth Editions
Unit 2a, The Works,
Colville Road, London W3 8BL, England
Design by Anikst Associates

British Library Cataloguing in Publication Data
 (data applied for)
ISBN 1 898592 15 2

Typeset by Anikst Design and Azimuth Editions
Printed by PJ Print, London

COVER. Detail from fig.34.Giovanni Battista Piranesi. Study for *Différentes vues de Pesto ...*, Plate XIII.
Temple of Neptune from within the peristyle at the west end looking south. Pen and brown ink with wash over red chalk.
c. 1777/8 (Sir John Soane's Museum).
FRONTISPIECE. Pietro Labruzzi. *Giovanni Battista Piranesi*, 1779. Oil on canvas (Museo di Roma).

Piranesi, Paestum & Soane

'…forget not Piranesi, who you may see in my name; he is full of matter, extravagant 'tis true, often absurd, but from his overflowings you may gather much information.'

This highly cautious advice was offered to the young John Soane in a letter given to him by Sir William Chambers (originally written by the latter for an earlier student traveller, Edward Stevens) when about to leave for his momentous Continental tour in 1778.[1] Already significantly influenced by Piranesi's potent etchings, Soane duly met the celebrated Venetian architect and engraver in Rome, within a few months of his death in November. From then onwards developed a profound yet complex artistic and intellectual relationship with Piranesi's concepts and revolutionary theories which covered the rest of Soane's career and helped to create, as with Robert Adam before him, a radical and highly distinctive style of design. As part of his fund of ideas, Soane not only acquired a remarkable group of Piranesi's drawings, as featured in this publication, together with a comprehensive set of his vast output of etched works, but collected a number of his restored classical antiquities. Most significant of all, however, was the way Soane exploited space, light and dramatic juxtapositions to arrange his Museum in the highly eclectic manner of Piranesi's architectural fantasies, with the same conscious intention to stimulate and inspire the creative imagination. Joseph Gandy's arresting views painted for Soane were to add further Piranesian dimensions to these arcane settings.

Giovanni Battista Piranesi
Although Piranesi was one of the supreme exponents of topographical engraving (his corpus comprises over a thousand separate etchings), his lifelong preoccupation with architecture is central to an understanding of his wide-ranging achievements.[2] Born in 1720, the son of a stonemason and master builder, he spent his first 20 years in Venice training in architecture and stage design, with strong influences from the local tradition of topographical art, represented by Canaletto, and the graphic fantasies of Marco Ricci and Tiepolo. Moving in 1740 to Rome, where he spent the rest of his life, a lack of practical architectural commissions led him to develop skills in etching souvenir views for the Grand Tour market.

His main creative energies, meanwhile, were concentrated on developing the architectural fantasy, or *capriccio*, as a vehicle for formal experiment and architectural reform, expressed in the plates of his first publication, *Prima Parte di Architetture e Prospettive* (1743).[3] Among these visionary compositions the *Bridge of Magnificence* or

Overleaf
FIG.1 Giovanni Battista Piranesi.
Bridge of Magnificence.
Etching (*Prima Parte,* Plate v, 1743).

FIG.2 Giovanni Battista Piranesi.
The Drawbridge.
Etching (*Carceri d'Invenzione,*
Plate vii, 1761).

Ponte magnifico con Logge, ed Archi eretto da un Imperatore Romano, nel mezzo si vede la Statua Equestre del medesimo. Questo ponte vien fuori di un arco d'un lato del Ponte che si unisce al sudetto, come si vede pure nel fondo un medesimo arco attaccato al principal P...

2

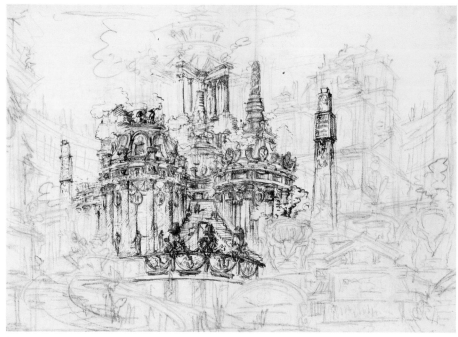

3

Left
FIG.3 Giovanni Battista Piranesi.
Imaginary architectural composition,
c. late 1740s.
Pen and brown ink with wash over
red chalk, 535 × 750 mm
(Sir John Soane's Museum,
Adam vol 26/163).

Facing page
FIG.4 Giovanni Battista Piranesi.
Imaginary architectural composition,
c. 1755.
Red and black chalk, brown ink and
brown wash, 385 × 530 mm
(Sir John Soane's Museum,
Adam vol 56/146).

Ponte Magnifico (FIG.1) was to exert a decisive influence on Soane's prize-winning *Triumphal Bridge* design for the Royal Academy's Gold Medal which, appropriately, was to lead to his travelling scholarship.[4] Moreover, Piranesi's celebrated suite of arcane prison fantasies, *Carceri d'Invenzione* (FIG.2), which first appeared around 1745 and was reissued in a highly influential version in 1761, had a considerable impact on Soane's complex spatial designs, not least within the Museum itself.[5] Through his etchings Piranesi was to exercise a seminal influence on European Neo-Classicism as well as through his personal contact with visiting artists, architects and patrons in Rome over the course of nearly four decades, among them Soane's first master, George Dance the Younger.[6] The impact of his radical ideas was to be particularly critical for Robert Adam who first met the Venetian in Rome during June 1755.[7] Writing back to his family in Scotland shortly after, Adam described the catalytic effect of Piranesi's mode of instruction as follows: 'so amazing and ingenious fancies [as] he has produced in the different plans of the temples, baths and palaces I never saw … are the greatest fund for inspiring and instilling invention in any lover of architecture that can be imagined. … he has told me that whatsoever I want of him he will do for me with pleasure, and is just doing two drawings for me which will be both singular and clever.'[8] He eventually returned to Britain with two fantasy drawings of the kind he describes Piranesi producing for him and which Soane may have acquired along with the Adam office collection in 1818 and 1833 respectively (FIGS 3, 4).[9]

4

From 1748 onwards Piranesi began his magisterial *Vedute di Roma*, a sequence of 135 plates, etched and issued individually or in groups throughout the rest of his career. The young Soane was presented with four of these when meeting Piranesi in the summer of 1778 – *The Pantheon*, *The Arch of Constantine*, *The Arch of Septimius Severus* and *The Tomb of Cecilia Metella* (FIG.5) – all of them buildings that contributed seminal ideas to Soane's later architectural designs.[10] Three of these prints were initially hung in the Breakfast Room in 12 Lincoln's Inn Fields in the 1790s. When Soane moved into No.13 in 1813 the prints were moved to that house, where from the mid-1820s all four hung in Soane's new Picture Room, grouped together behind the movable planes on its north side.[11] In these plates Piranesi transformed the traditional souvenir *veduta* as a conventional record by enlarging its scope for emotional as well as intellectual communication. By pushing the boundaries of etching technique to extremes and by exploiting scenographic perspective, he combined remarkable flights of imagination with a strongly practical understanding of ancient technology. Filled with a wealth of scholarly information, often amplified by extensive captions (keyed to the image by alphabetical letters), such images were to generate a highly charged emotional perception of the past which radically affected the art of topography and left an indelible perception of Roman antiquity on the European imagination.

Archaeology became of increasing concern to Piranesi during the 1750s. His four-volume treatise, *Le Antichità Romane* (1756), contained an unprecedented wealth of visual and technical information about the architecture, engineering and decorative vocabulary of ancient Rome. Apart from the comprehensive coverage of material, the 250 plates of the *Antichità* were to revolutionise the methods and range of technical archaeological illustrations.[12] In this respect they were to affect the effective and often morbidly dramatic way that Soane's exhibition perspectives, largely drawn by Joseph Gandy, were rendered. An outstanding example is the imaginary view of his recently constructed Rotunda in the Bank of England reduced to the melancholy grandeur of ancient ruins with antiquaries busily excavating the site (FIG.6).[13] The central two volumes of the *Antichità* were to prove of particular importance to Soane, being devoted to tomb and mausoleum design with a febrile fantasy as frontispiece to Volume Two, including

5

an inscribed tomb to Robert Adam (FIG.7).[14] Piranesi's monumental publication, directed to architects and designers rather than scholars and antiquarians, swiftly won him international recognition but also embroiled him, as a fervent protagonist of Rome, in the furious controversy provoked by the developing Greek Revival.[15] With the election of the Venetian pope, Clement XIII Rezzonico, the 1760s represented a golden age of patronage for Piranesi with financial support for a series of lavishly produced archaeological and polemical folios (including *Della Magnificenza ed Architettura de' Romani*, 1761, and *Il Campo Marzio dell'Antica Roma*, 1762, the latter being, significantly, dedicated to Adam).[16] In response to acerbic criticism of his theories by the French critic Mariette, in 1765 Piranesi issued the manifesto *Parere su l'Architettura*.[17] Taking

FIG.5 Giovanni Battista Piranesi. Tomb of Cecilia Metella, Rome. Etching *(Vedute di Roma*, c. 1764–5).

Facing page
FIG.6 John Soane.
Architectural Ruins: A Vision, drawn by Joseph Michael Gandy, 1798. Pen and watercolour, 660 × 1020 mm (Sir John Soane's Museum).

6

the form of a debate between two architects, this advocated a highly idiosyncratic and eclectic system of design inspired by ancient Rome in contrast to the radically astringent taste supported by the Greek Revivalists. By this time Piranesi had already moved beyond the narrow academic squabbles of the Graeco-Roman controversy to promote a contemporary style formed by combining ideas from a range of ancient cultures – Greek as well as Roman, Etruscan and even Egyptian. The significance of this cultural cross-fertilisation for Soane, as much as for Adam before him, cannot be overestimated.

Meanwhile, through the Pope and members of the Rezzonico family, Piranesi had received commissions to carry out these ideas in designing a monumental tribune for S. Giovanni in Laterano (unrealised) and reconstructing the Order of Malta's church

in Rome, S. Maria del Priorato (executed 1764–5).[18] Soane was to acquire among his collection of Adam material three unattributed record drawings of Piranesi's designs for the church: one for the façade (FIG.8), displaying its sophisticated linear collage of antique motifs derived from Roman and Etruscan sources, another for the highly eccentric high altar within (FIG.9), and a third, of its entrance screen, encrusted with symbolic reliefs, in the adjacent Piazza de' Cavalieri di Malta (FIG.10).[19] During the 1760s Piranesi also produced furnished interiors for the Rezzonicos, complex marble chimneypieces and a pioneering painted interior in the Egyptian taste for the English coffee house in Rome (almost certainly seen by Soane on his tour but later destroyed). Many of these works were to be illustrated in Piranesi's internationally influential

8   9   10

Facing page

FIG.7 Giovanni Battista Piranesi.
Imaginary view of the Via Appia.
Etching (*Antichità Romane*, II, 1756).

FIG.8 After Giovanni Battista Piranesi.
Façade, plan and elevation of
S. Maria del Priorato, Rome.
Pen and grey washes on tracing paper,
304 × 190 mm (Sir John Soane's
Museum, Adam vol 27/48).

FIG.9 After Giovanni Battista Piranesi.
Partial elevation of the high altar,
S. Maria del Priorato, Rome.
Pen over pencil, 307 × 193 mm (Sir John
Soane's Museum, Adam vol 26/177).

FIG.10 After Giovanni Battista Piranesi.
Elevation of the entrance screen to
S. Maria del Priorato, Rome.
Pen and grey washes, 121 × 270 mm
(Sir John Soane's Museum,
Adam vol 26/178).

testament of design, *Diverse Maniere d'Adornare i Cammini* (1769), which contained a wide range of his extremely original designs for chimneypieces and furniture, providing a further mine of inspiration for sympathetic designers such as Soane.[20]

With the decline of Rezzonico patronage after the death of Clement XIII in 1769, Piranesi's last years involved the production of highly imaginatively restored antiquities, largely for the British Grand Tour market, which were displayed in his 'museo' or showrooms in Palazzo Tomati, close to the top of the Spanish Steps, where Soane was to meet the artist in 1778. Many of these elaborate fabrications (the more extreme being termed '*pasticcios*' by Piranesi's critics), together with works from other Roman collections, were depicted in the plates of the composite publication, *Vasi, Candelabri, Cippi, Sarcofagi…*, issued in the same year and which provided a popular repertoire of ornamental detail for Soane's generation.[21] A number of modestly restored works in marble found their way into Soane's collection to add to the sepulchral atmosphere of the Museum's Crypt. These included a rectangular cinerary urn, illustrated in the *Vasi* (FIG.11), an urn with winged genii and a capital with dolphins, both also illustrated in the *Vasi*, and a fragment of an Egyptian foliate capital which Piranesi had illustrated in his first compilation of archaeological material, *Trofei di Ottaviano Augusto*, published in 1753 as 'useful to painters, sculptors and architects'.[22]

The communication of powerful and emotive architectural ideas continued to be of central concern to Piranesi right to the end of his highly productive life. Although suffering from the advanced stages of a serious bladder complaint, towards the end of 1777 Piranesi made an arduous expedition to the remote malarial marshes in the Bay of Salerno, some 100 kilometres south of Naples, to record the three majestic Greek Doric temples at Paestum (FIG.12). He was accompanied by his 19-year-old son

13

Francesco and his assistant Benedetto Mori, as well as the architect Augusto Rosa, who was to take measurements in order to make souvenir models in cork.[23] Eventually returning with a set of exceptionally detailed drawings, 15 of which Soane was later to acquire (FIGS 19–34), Piranesi began to etch a suite of 20 *vedute* and a frontispiece which were to form his last work, the folio *Différentes vues de quelques restes de trois grands édfices qui subsistent encore dans le milieu de l'ancienne ville de Pesto ….*[24] While this received the papal imprimatur, authorising its publication, on 15 September 1778, sadly Piranesi died soon after, on 9 November, leaving behind an unfinished set of

11

plates to be completed and issued by Francesco later the same year. The latter and his siblings, Angelo, Pietro and Laura, who had all been trained in etching by their father, continued the family business at Palazzo Tomati. Shortly after Giovanni Battista's death, the family appear to have commissioned a portrait in oils of him as founder of the business by Pietro Labruzzi, in which the architect, as a Cavaliere di Sperone d'Oro, is shown holding the sketch of the Paestum frontispiece together with his drawing instruments (FRONTISPIECE).[25] This painting, which closely follows Joseph Nollekens's bust of Giovanni Battista, carved around 1760 for the Accademia di San Luca in Rome, also shows a portion of the large marble candelabrum (now in the Louvre) which had been ingeniously assembled from antique fragments and destined by the designer for his tomb.[26]

FIG.12 Antonio Joli. *The Temples of Paestum*, c. 1758. Oil on canvas (The Duke of Buccleuch).

Paestum and the Greek Revival

By the time that Piranesi drew the temples at Paestum in 1777, the Greek Revival had already developed from its initial stage of offering a novel challenge to Roman classicism, during the early 1750s, towards being an aggressive movement of moral fervour and artistic orthodoxy.[27] The defence of Greece had been introduced early in the 18th century by French theorists, such as Frézier and De Cordemoy, as an offshoot from the protracted quarrel between the Ancients and Moderns. However, it fell to the Jesuit Marc-Antoine Laugier in his *Essai sur l'architecture* of 1753 – a work much valued

by Soane, who possessed 10 copies – to create the greatest impact with a specific philosophy of design.[28] Assessing architecture on the fundamental principle of the imitation of Nature, as represented by Vitruvius' description of the rustic hut as a functional paradigm, Laugier asserted that Greek buildings possessed a truthfulness in structure and simplicity of form which had ultimately been debased and corrupted by Roman designers and their later followers. This introduced a particularly potent idea, comparable to Rousseau's conviction that one should return to the beginnings of human history to discover the norm by which the present should be guided. While the writings and influence of the great German art historian Winckelmann from the mid-1750s onwards, if largely confined to painting and sculpture, was to reinforce this view, a series of archaeological investigations and publications about surviving Greek buildings began to appear during that decade. Although the British architects Stuart and Revett surveyed the buildings of Athens between 1751 and 1755, the first volume of their *Antiquities of Athens* did not appear until 1762, by which time the Frenchman Le Roy had anticipated them with his more superficial book, *Les Ruines des plus beaux monuments de la Grèce*, in 1758. This latter work, with its extravagant claims for Greek originality, more than any other, provoked Piranesi's wrath. He swiftly abandoned his former contacts with the French Academy in Rome, as a growing focus of philhellenism, in favour of visiting architects from Britain such as Chambers, Robert and James Adam, Mylne and Dance, with their more pragmatic viewpoint. The French bias towards the Greek side of the ensuing debate had already been indicated as early as 1750 when the temples at Paestum were among the sites specially visited during the famous educational visit to Italy of Madame de Pompadour's brother, the Marquis de Marigny, as Surintendant des Bâtiments designate, accompanied by the engraver Cochin, the architect Soufflot and his assistant Dumont.

13b

FIGS 13 a–b Domenico Padiglione. Model of the Temple of Neptune, Paestum, after 1802. Cork with terracotta capitals, on a mahogany base (Sir John Soane's Museum).

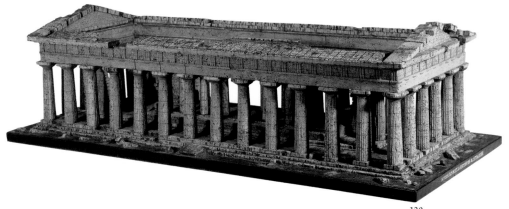

13a

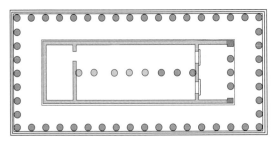

14a

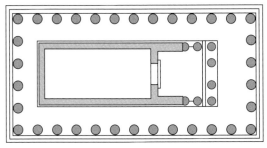

14b

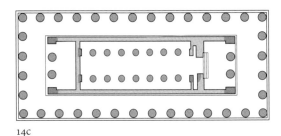

14c

Above
FIGS 14a–c Plans of the three temples at Paestum (not to the same scale).
(a) Basilica (Temple of Hera I).
(b) Temple of Juno (Athena).
(c) Temple of Neptune (Hera II).

Poseidonia, or Paestum, had been originally founded by Greek settlers around 600 BC at a particularly effective commercial location on the Tyrrhenian coast for trade in Magna Graecia. The city underwent a period of great prosperity from approximately 560 to 440 BC when each of the three temples was constructed at a different time, their respective dedications only being established by recent excavations.[29] Towards the end of the 5th century, around 420–410 BC, the city was taken over by Lucanian Samnites and, in 273 BC, they in turn were supplanted by the Romans who founded a colony there and changed the city's name to the present one. Of the three main sanctuaries the Temple of Hera I (known as the Basilica in Piranesi's time) of *circa* 550–530 BC, stands close to the southern end of the original city area and has a well-preserved peristyle with 9 columns on each end and 18 to either side (FIG.14a). A single colonnade runs down the middle of the former cella or internal walled space which housed a cult image and was entered through a porch at the east end (pronaos) with three columns between pilasters. No roof, cella walls or pediments survive, while the Doric columns are noted for their visibly bulging character, shown by the exaggerated entasis or swelling effect. At a considerable distance to the north is the Temple of Athena (formerly known as that of Ceres and, in Piranesi's time, ascribed to Juno), of *circa* 500 BC, which has a peristyle of 6 by 13 columns and is distinctive for its use of the Ionic order in the pronaos, within the colonnade (FIG.14b). Parts of its two pediments remain, together with the complete peristyle, but it lacks a roof and walls to the cella. Latest in date and only a few hundred metres away on a slight rise in the ground north of the earliest sanctuary of Hera I is the Temple of Hera II (known to Piranesi as that of Neptune or Poseidon, and most recently ascribed by certain archaeologists to Apollo), of *circa* 450 BC (FIG.14c). This is by far the largest and grandest of the three structures, its design showing considerable debts to that of the Temple of Zeus at Olympia, of *circa* 470 BC, and is among the best preserved Greek temples on this scale surviving anywhere. It not only retains its Doric peristyle complete (6 by 14 columns) but most of its two pediments and a striking portion of the two-tiered double colonnade within the original cella, the walls of which have largely disappeared. Also surviving within the peristyle at the east end is the pronaos consisting of two columns between pilasters, balanced by a similar porch, or opisthodomos, at the west end.

While the equally striking Greek temples in Sicily at Agrigento, Segesta and Selinunte were also explored during the mid-18th century, those at Paestum were relatively more accessible to visitors attracted by the excavations at Herculaneum and Pompeii and were to be recorded in more publications than all the Sicilian examples put together.[30] While first recorded by Costantino Gatta in a map of 1732, the effective discovery of the Paestum temples in their desolate setting in 1746 is attributed to the architect Mario Gioffredo, and early measured drawings, undertaken for Count Felice Gazzola, commander of the Neapolitan artillery, were engraved in Paris in 1752.[31] One of the earliest accounts of the temples in English was made the following year by Frederick North, Earl of Guilford, whose substantial description was among the first to convey that sense of shock to eyes accustomed to Palladian elegance. As he observed about the Temple of Neptune:

The Columns are of an ancient Dorick order & seem to have been made at ye time, when that order was coming out of its original rough state & forming itself to that beauty it afterwards attained. They are short, clumsy & ill-shaped. Their diameter is much smaller at ye top, than ye bottom; Their Capitals are very flat: They are fluted, but ye flutings are very coarse. I think they resemble in shape pretty much those props, on which our peasants in England sometimes put their corn, to prevent its being eaten by vermin.[32]

Something of the wildness and sublimity of the setting is evoked in one of the earliest paintings of the site, made by Antonio Joli for John, Lord Brudenell during his Grand Tour stay in Naples between 1756 and 1758 (FIG.12).[33] By this time Soufflot had carried out a thorough survey during de Marigny's expedition in 1750 which eventually resulted in the first comprehensive publication on Paestum by his pupil, Gabriel-Pierre-Martin Dumont, partly plagiarising Gazzola's pioneering work. Dumont's *Suite de plans … de trois temples antiques … de Paestum* appeared in Paris in 1764, followed by an improved edition in 1769, *Les Ruines de Paestum* (FIG.15). From the 1760s, as the cult of the primitive developed, reinforced by radical Neo-Classical theories, a considerable quantity of views, survey drawings and publications of Paestum began to appear. However, not all contemporary visitors found the experience inspiring; James Adam, for instance, on a visit in November 1761, reported that he had seen 'the famous antiquities so much talked of late as wonders, but which, curiosity apart, dont merit half the time and trouble they have cost me. They are of an early, an inelegant and unenriched Doric, that afford no detail and scarcely produce two good views. So much for Paestum.'[34] Tastes, however, were beginning to change by the close of the decade and more technical studies were to be published, the most notable and the most accurate to date being Thomas Major's *Ruins of Paestum* of 1768; Soane later acquired a group of this author's preparatory drawings and etchings along with the book.[35] Three-dimensional souvenirs were also produced and, during the late 1760s, Vincenzo Brenna made cork models of the temples, as well as a series of measured drawings, for the leading British collector of classical antiquities, Charles Townley, after they had surveyed the site together. Similarly, as mentioned earlier, Augusto Rosa joined Piranesi's expedition in 1777 to produce such works, an example of which may be the solitary model of the Temple of Neptune in the Soane Museum. Such models were still popular a few decades later when Domenico Padiglione made models of all three temples, around 1805, and Soane was to acquire a set of these from the collection of his pupil John Sanders around 1826 (FIG.13).[36]

FIG.15 Gabriel-Pierre-Martin Dumont. Interior of the Temple of Neptune, Paestum, from the west. Engraving (*Les Ruines de Paestum*, 1769).

Bichard Scul.

15

Piranesi and Paestum

It is extremely likely that Giovanni Battista Piranesi had visited Paestum before his intensive survey in 1777 with Francesco and colleagues, since earlier in that decade he had begun to make a considerable number of drawings in the newly excavated parts of Pompeii (FIG.16), some 60 kilometres to the north. These latter were intended for illustrations to a projected volume on Magna Graecia which Francesco was ultimately to etch and publish, posthumously, as *Antiquités de la Grande Grèce*. While the surviving sketches, strangely bleak and coarsely executed, may reflect the dearth of inspiration in a site devoid of the enlivening forms of foliage and human activity, they indicate a development in Piranesi's style towards a greater preoccupation with stark effects of sublimity and powerful tonal contrasts. By the mid-1770s, as a result of the rapidly grow-ing interest in Paestum, Giovanni Battista clearly felt the need to record what amounted to the most significant classical structures under discussion located in Italy, and, accord-ing to his earliest biographer, J.G. Legrand, had been inspired to make a special expedition by seeing some drawings of them in Rome.[37] While the published text and substantial captions were to make no direct reference to issues of the Graeco-Roman debate, Piranesi implied that the temples' grandeur was due to being erected on Italian soil and took considerable pains to stress how these monuments demonstrated the freedom from rigid rules and powers of invention shown by the ancient architects, as discussed in his *Parere su l'Architettura* some fourteen years earlier.[38] The fact that the ensuing text and captions were to be in French rather than Italian (and this is likely to have been Francesco's decision more than his father's) may have been a response to the strong French commitment to the Greek Revival as much as to the international audience intended.

Since Giovanni Battista was only too aware of his mortality and the strong likeli-hood of having to hand over the unfinished work to Francesco, who clearly lacked his own experience and skills, the surviving 17 preparatory drawings for the 21 plates of Paestum – 15 acquired by Soane (FIGS 19–32, 34) and two others in Paris and Amsterdam respectively (FIGS 17, 18) – are unusually detailed, contrary to his normal practice, and are approximately the same size as the published plates.[39] The fact that, with the exception of the study for Plate II, they are drawn in the same direction as the etchings, however, is characteristic of Piranesi, who hardly ever used a compositional drawing to translate mechanically a complete composition direct to the copper plate, as the reverse image enabled less accomplished artists to do. While the finish of certain of these Paestum drawings is relatively incomplete (notably that for Plate IX, FIG.26), most of the relatively few compositional studies that survive before Piranesi's closing years tend to be summary outlines, being sufficient to lay out the perspectival structure on his plates.[40] Indeed, once the surface of the plate was waxed and blackened, the sharp point of the etching needle acted freely in the manner of a pen in providing a formidable variety of touches to register the different properties of materials and textures as well

FIG.16 Giovanni Battista Piranesi. Study for *Vue de la Taverne de Pompeia*, c. 1777/8. Pen, ink and wash (British Museum).

16

Overleaf
FIG.17 (right) Giovanni Battista Piranesi.
Study for *Différentes vues de Pesto …*,
Plate I. View of the three temples from
the south. Pen and brown ink with
washes over black chalk, c. 1777/8
(Bibliothèque Nationale, Paris).

FIG.18 (left) Giovanni Battista Piranesi.
Study for *Différentes vues de Pesto …*,
Plate XIX. View of the Temple of Juno
from the south-west. Pen and brown ink
with wash over red chalk, c. 1777/8
(Rijksmuseum, Amsterdam).

as to suggest the play of light on forms and surfaces. Since he possessed an extremely
retentive visual memory, Piranesi felt that a finished preparatory drawing would thus
undermine the immediacy and spontaneity of etching detail straight on to the plate
itself. According to his earliest biographer, J.G. Legrand, Piranesi once explained to the
ruin painter Hubert Robert that: '… the drawing isn't just what you see on the paper,
I agree, but it is totally in my head and you will see it on the plate.' Legrand went on to
say: 'Piranesi never produced finished sketches, a rough study in chalk, reworked with
pen or brush and even then only in parts, being sufficient to secure his ideas. It is almost
impossible to distinguish his thoughts on paper because it is nothing but a chaos from
which he only extracted a few elements for his plate with consummate skill.'[41] It is necessary to labour this point because in these Paestum drawings we are given a unique
opportunity to see his full creative process at work. Putting aside the problematic con-
tribution of Francesco for the moment and comparing, for instance, the original drawing
for Plate XIII (*Interior of the Temple of Neptune within the peristyle at the west end*) (FIG.34)
with the etched plate (FIG.35), the resemblances in technique are particularly striking.
In the drawing, after pale washes of brown and Indian inks were applied over lightly
black chalk outlines, details were then drawn with delicate pen work in brown ink.
The foreground was next worked over in line and wash with deep brown and heavier

17

Indian inks. Final reinforcements were made with a wash of dark Indian ink, usually in the foreground, but occasionally in the middle distance as well. While it is clear that the majority of figures were added by Piranesi after the architectural elements were resolved in outline, certain of them were clearly anticipated at an earlier stage and integrated with the architecture. This highly complex drawing technique closely reflects the repeated bitings by acid in the etching process itself and constitutes a *tour de force* in evoking the full atmospheric impression of these heroic structures.

As Hylton Thomas expressed it in his pioneering study of the artist's draughtsmanship, Piranesi achieved a fine balance between 'the solidity of form and beauty of surface, between the tectonic and the sensuous'.[42] Few other topographical engravers could rival his legendary skills in conveying the powerful formal abstraction of stone structures with the play of light during the passage of the sun and the nuances of atmospheric perspective, the latter qualities significantly being inherited from Piranesi's early Venetian training. These elusive properties could only be achieved by careful analysis of the changing effects of light and of weather conditions. Legrand drew attention to the artist's painstaking approach to his subject matter in this respect:

The truthfulness and vigour of his effects, the precise projection of his shadows and their transparency along with certain liberties taken in this respect, even indications of colour, were all based on daily observation. This was equally true whether in normal conditions, or under the full glare of the sun, or by moonlight when the masses of the

18

FIG.19 Giovanni Battista Piranesi. Study for *Différentes vues de Pesto…*, Plate II. The Basilica from the east. Pen with black ink and grey washes over black chalk and graphite, 480 × 685 mm. c. 1777/8 (Sir John Soane's Museum).

FIG.20 Giovanni Battista Piranesi. Study for *Différentes vues de Pesto …*, Plate III. The Basilica showing part of the west peristyle with the other two temples in the distance. Pen with brown ink and grey washes over black chalk and graphite, 510 × 685 mm. c. 1777/8 (Sir John Soane's Museum).

FIG.21 Giovanni Battista Piranesi. Study for *Différentes vues de Pesto …*, Plate IV. The Basilica from the north with the corner of Temple of Neptune in the foreground. Pen with brown ink and wash over black chalk and graphite with traces of red chalk, 481 × 678 mm. c. 1777/8 (Sir John Soane's Museum).

20

19

21

23

FIG.22 Giovanni Battista Piranesi.
Study for *Différentes vues de Pesto …*, Plate V.
The interior of the Basilica, looking north, showing the
pronaos, with the Temple of Neptune in the distance.
Pen with brown ink and grey and brown washes over
black chalk with traces of red chalk, 516 × 483 mm.
c. 1777/8 (Sir John Soane's Museum).

FIG.23 Giovanni Battista Piranesi.
Study for *Différentes vues de Pesto …*, Plate VI.
The Basilica looking west with the *pronaos* in the
foreground and the Temple of Neptune to the right.
Pen with black and brown ink and washes over black
chalk with some white chalk highlights, 485 × 691 mm.
c. 1777/8 (Sir John Soane's Museum).

22

24

FIG.24 Giovanni Battista Piranesi.
Study for *Différentes vues de Pesto ...*,
Plate VIII. The interior of the Basilica,
looking north, with the *pronaos* to
the right and the Temple of Neptune
in the distance on the left.
Pen with brown ink and wash
over black chalk with some red chalk,
502 × 685 mm.
c. 1777/8 (Sir John Soane's Museum).

FIG.25 Giovanni Battista Piranesi. Study for *Différentes vues de Pesto …*, Plate VII. The interior of the Basilica, looking east, with a section of the south peristyle, the central columns of the *cella* and the *pronaos* in the distance. Pen with black and brown ink and ink washes over black chalk and graphite, 482 × 687 mm.
c. 1777/8 (Sir John Soane's Museum).

26

28   27

FIG.26 (previous page, top right)
Giovanni Battista Piranesi.
Study for *Différentes vues de Pesto ...*,
Plate IX. The interior of the Basilica,
looking east, with the three surviving
columns of the *cella* and the *pronaos*
in the distance.
Pen with brown ink and grey wash
over black chalk or graphite with
traces of red chalk, 501 × 686 mm.
c. 1777/8 (Sir John Soane's Museum).

FIG.27 (previous page, bottom right)
Giovanni Battista Piranesi.
Study for *Différentes vues de Pesto ...*,
Plate X. The Temple of Neptune from
the north-east with the Basilica
to the left.
Pen with black and brown ink and
washes over black chalk or graphite
with traces of red chalk and white
chalk highlights, 502 × 693 mm.
c. 1777/8 (Sir John Soane's Museum).

FIG.28 (previous page, left)
Giovanni Battista Piranesi.
Study for *Différentes vues de Pesto ...*,
Plate XI. The Temple of Neptune
from the south-west.
Pen with brown ink and wash
over black chalk with some graphite,
480 × 687 mm.
c. 1777/8 (Sir John Soane's Museum).

FIG.29 Giovanni Battista Piranesi.
Study for *Différentes vues de Pesto ...*,
Plate XII. The interior of the
Temple of Neptune from the
north-east (with the peristyle partly
removed) showing the *pronaos* and
internal colonnades.
Pen with black and brown ink and
washes over black chalk or graphite,
480 × 686 mm.
c. 1777/8 (Sir John Soane's Museum).

29

30

31

FIG.30 Giovanni Battista Piranesi.
Study for *Différentes vues de Pesto …*,
Plate XVI. The interior of the
Temple of Neptune from within the
cella area looking east and showing the
internal superimposed colonnades.
Pen with black and brown ink and
washes over black chalk and graphite,
500 × 682 mm.
c. 1777/8 (Sir John Soane's Museum).

FIG.31 Giovanni Battista Piranesi.
Study for *Différentes vues de Pesto …*,
Plate XIV. The interior of the
Temple of Neptune, looking south-west,
showing the inner side of the
opisthodomos, or rear porch.
Pen with black and brown ink and
washes over graphite and black chalk
with a letter A in red chalk on the
central figure and a vertical red chalk
line top centre, 496 × 686 mm.
c. 1777/8 (Sir John Soane's Museum).

32

FIGS 32 (left) and 33 (right) Giovanni Battista Piranesi. Study for *Différentes vues de Pesto …*, Plate XVII. The Temple of Neptune looking through the peristyle from the north-west corner, showing the internal colonnades and the Basilica in the distance. Pen with black and brown ink and wash over black chalk and graphite, 510 × 687 mm. c. 1777/8 (Sir John Soane's Museum).

FIG.34 Giovanni Battista Piranesi. Study for *Différentes vues de Pesto ...*, Plate XIII.
The Temple of Neptune from within the peristyle at the west end looking south.
Pen with brown ink and wash over black chalk with traces of red chalk and white chalk highlights, 484 × 687 mm.
c. 1777/8 (Sir John Soane's Museum).

FIG.35 Giovanni Battista Piranesi. The Temple of Neptune from within the peristyle at the west end looking south.
Etching (*Différentes vues de Pesto ...*, Plate XIII, 1778).

35

architecture seemed to increase their effects of strength and solidity as well as a softness and harmony often far superior to the brilliance of daylight. He learned these effects by heart from studying them both close at hand and from afar and at all times ...[43]

In the Paestum drawings and plates, one is continually aware of each temple's setting on the site, whether it is the expanses of sky above the low horizon looking west towards the Gulf of Salerno, or the mountainous prospects beyond the undulating, arid landscape in the other directions. Times of day are also varied in order for the strong sunlight and shadows to make their own contributions to conveying mood as well as information.

Much of the potency as well as the wealth of spatial information in Piranesi's *vedute* came from his early training in stage design; an essential ingredient in his art which he shared with his fellow Venetian Canaletto. Quite apart from the dramatic effects of lighting, early on in his career Giovanni Battista had learnt the potential of the Bibiena family's compositional device – *scena per angolo* – a revolutionary concept whereby the traditional centre viewpoint in stage sets was abandoned in favour of several diagonal axes, each of which enabled further vistas to open, thus creating a spatial structure of the richest complexity. This was used to powerful effect in the *Carceri d'Invenzione* (FIG.2) as well as a large number of the interior scenes in the *Vedute di Roma* and

34

archaeological interior views. With these scenographic and informative factors in mind, the documentation of the three Paestum temples in terms of their components, such as the surrounding colonnades or peristyles, as well as their surviving internal features and, most importantly, their relation to one another, were conveyed in the same manner by a series of carefully selected perspectives.[44]

Characteristic of Piranesi's awareness of the broader landscape context, a general view of all three temples from the south-west was chosen for Plate I, as represented by the study now in the Bibliothèque Nationale (FIG.17).[45] As the numbered sequence of etchings suggests, the Basilica and Temple of Neptune were given greatest attention and their close proximity exploited for complex vistas, in the absence of cella walls, through their colonnades. The Basilica (Hera I), with its highly primitive columns, was to receive eight specific views, three from different external points and five within the space, all corresponding to his drawings at the Soane (FIGS.19–26). In the case of FIG.25, which looks east into the remains of the cella space and shows three surviving columns of the internal colonnade, in order to do this effectively Piranesi adopted a technique (used earlier in certain of his *Vedute di Roma*) of deliberately cutting out part of the external (south) colonnade which would have obscured this feature.[46]

Next in order, but unquestionably of the maximum interest for Piranesi and his team, was the Temple of Neptune (Hera II), which was to be given nine plates. First, came a general external view of its most complete appearance from the north-east, with a glimpse of the Basilica to the left (FIG.27), together with a powerful close perspective of the southern range of the peristyle from the south-west (FIG.28). Because of the temple's exceptionally fascinating interior with porches at both ends and surviving portions of the two internal colonnades with superimposed columns (which had originally supported the roof of the cella), six interior views were produced and an additional one was used as the frontispiece. Missing from the Soane drawings for this particular group (FIGS 29–32, 33 detail, 34) are studies for Plate XV and the frontispiece (FIG.36).

Only three plates were eventually to be published of the third structure, the Temple of Juno (Athena), which was situated at a distance from the others at the northern end of the site (Plates XVIII–XX). Two are taken from the south-east and south-west respectively, and the final one at close range from the north-west reveals the interior by means of artificially omitting at least three of the columns of the northern colonnade, as in the manner of Plate VII (FIG.25). While none of the drawings for this last temple is represented among the Soane group, a study for Plate XIX survives in the Rijksmuseum, Amsterdam (FIG.18), and, whether or not other drawings were made, it is possible that more plates were intended but abandoned on account of Giovanni Battista's rapidly declining health.[47]

Vûe des restes interieurs du Temple de Neptune. Nous ne nous etendrons pas a donner un detail de ces morceaux, parce qu'ils seront bien detaillés, et bien specifiés dans les Planches suivantes. Dans ce Frontispice nous les avons dessinés tels qu'ils existent afin d'en presenter un grand appareil uni a d'autres amas de ruines, que nous donnerons ci apres dans les Planches. Les Voyageurs connoisseurs auront que par raport a l'Architecture Grecque des Temples bâtis dans l'Ordre Dorique, ceux de Pesto sont superieurs en beauté a ceux qu'on voit en Sicile, et dans la Grece, et que sans se donner la peine, et la fatigue de longs voyages, ceux ci peuvent suffire pour contenter la curiosité, et qu'enfin cette grande, et majestueuse Architecture donne en son genre l'Idée la plus parfaite de ce bel Art.

36

Function and attribution: the problem of the Paestum Drawings

The fact that the surviving 17 Paestum drawings, which include the two in Paris and Amsterdam (Figs 17, 18), show a number of inconsistencies from one another, in terms of technique, finish and composition, has raised considerable questions about their function as well as their authorship. Their provenance, moreover, still remains uncertain and Soane's group can only be traced to his possession by 1818, no evidence having so far come to light as to exactly when, where and under what circumstances

37

38

FIG.37 Giovanni Battista Piranesi. The interior of the Temple of Neptune from the north-east with the *pronaos*. Proof etching (*Différentes vues de Pesto ...*, Plate XII, 1778). (British Museum).

FIG.38 Giovanni Battista Piranesi. The interior of the Temple of Neptune from the north-east with the *pronaos*. Etching (*Différentes vues de Pesto ...*, Plate XII, published version, 1778).

he obtained them. By 1820 they were hanging in his bedroom in 13 Lincoln's Inn Fields, according to a drawing in the Winterthur Collection, Delaware, and were then transferred to the Picture Room where they were hung during Soane's lifetime, not as a group but distributed among the other prints, watercolours and paintings.[48]

While, with the exception of the study for Plate II (FIG.19), all of the images are drawn in the same direction as the etchings and are slightly larger in scale than the latter, some of them have marked differences from the finished plates, especially in terms of the figures, the staffage of animals, foliage, etc. and, occasionally, the apparent incompleteness of certain compositions. Others match the plates closely in almost every respect and some scholars have suggested the possibility that these were actually copied from the latter after the etching process in order to replace missing studies, although for several reasons this seems unlikely.

One of these identical drawings is related to a completely etched second version of Plate XII, the interior of the Temple of Neptune from the north-east with the pronaos. An extremely rare proof pull in the British Museum of this plate (with a blank scroll, within the plate area, awaiting a caption) shows the identical scene, except taken from a slightly lower view-point and further to the right, with completely different figures in the foreground (FIG.37).[49] In the second version of the plate which replaced it in the published folio (FIG.38), the central group with a man drawing, watched by a colleague leaning on a fragment, is replaced by a group of three men, the middle figure standing and two seated, one of the latter playing with an excited dog. To their left is added another figure sitting against a column (a similar one seated against the pronaos column in the first plate version is now omitted), and to the right the two active figures in the earlier version are replaced by a meditative figure with a stick, who contemplates a donkey across a column drum. In the later etching, as in many other of the Soane drawings, more figures and animals are added, along with foliage, and changes are made to the sky. While the replaced plate could be accounted for by damage to the first version, as Jonathan Scott has convincingly suggested, the second etching has enough minor but telling additions to enrich the composition outlined in the relevant Soane drawing (FIG.29) in order to justify the latter's preparatory function for Piranesi.[50]

The role of Francesco Piranesi

The marked differences between the figure style of the first version of the etched Plate XII and that of the published version, together with its related Soane drawing, opens up what is probably the most controversial issue in Piranesi studies; namely, the respective contributions of Giovanni Battista and the young Francesco, both to the drawings as well as the published edition on Paestum.[51] For instance, in the first version of Plate XII (FIG.37) the etched foreground figures are angular, lithe and fully integrated within the graphic composition; several are markedly animated in the act of urgent enquiry as if involved in Piranesi's final expedition to the site. However, in the published plate (FIG.38) the principal figures possess a far more stocky physique and, for all their placid, elegiac character, frequently appear to relate less successfully in the composition to their physical environment. It is well established thatafter Giovanni Battista's death in November 1778, Francesco was to finish off his father's incomplete plates, signing the last two (XIX and XX) as well as the Frontispiece (FIG.36).[52] This latter has a prominent group of these somewhat awkwardly placed figures, at least one (FIG.39) being added to what appears to be the missing original design for this plate, partially shown in the corner of the Labruzzi portrait (FRONTISPIECE).[53]

By the last ten years of his prolific life, Giovanni Battista had clearly begun to consider the problem of completing a formidable programme of projects and had ensured that of his five surviving children not only his eldest son Francesco, born in 1758, but also Laura and Pietro were trained in the print-making business. Franceso also appears to have received some training in the French Academy in Rome as well as from his father, but no firm date for any executed work has so far come to light before he completed and published the Paestum etchings in 1778. If Legrand's biography can be relied upon, and this was largely based on the Piranesi family's own account of life with their father, Giovanni Battista seems to have found it hard to delegate. According to the Frenchman, Giovanni Battista 'was always afraid that the youth of his [eldest] son would prevent the continuity of order established in his workshop in which many draughtsmen and engravers worked under his immediate direction, each one carrying out the task he had been given, but Piranesi always kept the difficult parts himself and maintained the overall control'.[54]

Owing to a current lack of evidence, our knowledge of Francesco's early artistic activities, both in drawing as well as etching, is extremely problematic. One of the only datable examples of his drawing style appears to be a design in Berlin for an unrealised plate in which he dedicates a projected work, incorporating the antiquities of Paestum with others in the region, to the King of Naples, Ferdinand IV (FIG.40).[55] The pedestrian quality of its draughtsmanship and clumsy composition suggest not only a date close to the appearance of the Paestum volume but tend to confirm Francesco's lack of proficiency to make the kind of independent contributions to the Paestum drawings suggested by some authorities.

In the decade following the publication of the Paestum volume Francesco was to complete several other works initiated by his father including a six-plate map of Hadrian's Villa, Tivoli (1781), a double plate map of the Emissarium of Lake Fucino (1791) and additional plates to Giovanni Battista's existing publications, *Archi Trionfali*, *Trofei*, *Vedute di Roma*, and *Le Antichità Romane*. As a supplement to the last work, Francesco issued the two volumes of the *Tempi Antichi* (1780, 1790) and his other new works included *Il Teatro di Ercolano* (1783), *Monumenti degli Scipioni*

39

FIG.39 Detail from FIG.36 of the piping figure added by Francesco Piranesi to the etched frontispiece.

FIG.40 Francesco Piranesi. Study for a dedication plate to Ferdinand IV of a proposed folio, *Monumenta Paestana*. Pen and brown ink with grey wash, c. 1778 (Kunstbibliothek, Berlin).

40

(1785), and a group of *vedute* from the Naples region, etched from drawings by J.L. Desprez. Apart from an anthology of sculpture in the *Collection des plus belles statues de Rome* (1786), to consolidate these achievements in 1792 he produced a complete catalogue of the Piranesi firm's productions and classified all the plates with Roman numerals. Apart from selling the remainder of his father's collection of antiquities to Gustav III of Sweden in 1783, he was appointed the king's agent for the fine arts in Italy and in 1794 became the Swedish consul in Naples. Returning to Rome four years later, he got caught up in revolutionary politics, and served, together with Pietro, as an official in the short-lived Republic. With the arrival of the British and Neapolitan forces there in 1800, the two brothers fled with the rest of the Piranesi family to Paris (taking their father's plates, drawings and monumental funerary candelabrum) where they set up business. Francesco issued the bulk of the firm's works in a handsome new edition of 27 volumes between 1800 and 1807, as well as the three-volume *Antiquités de la Grande Grèce* (1804–7) which included plates based on his father's Pompeii drawings (including a map of the current excavations). Even in the latest of these etched works, there are few signs of more than average graphic skills. Meanwhile, the corpus of

Giovanni Battista's original copper plates, for all their benefits from decades of reissue, were becoming out of fashion with the new tastes for a greater if somewhat prosaic attention to archaeological fact. After Francesco's death in 1810 the business was wound up and, after further use in France by another print firm, Firmin Didot, the complete set of surviving plates was eventually returned to Rome in 1839 to be deposited in what is now the Calcografia Nazionale.

The Piranesi figure style

While accepting that the architecture in both drawings and etchings still shows the incomparable hand of the father, some scholars have concluded that Francesco was not only responsible for most figures in the etchings but had also added these earlier, to the preparatory drawings themselves. Since throughout the majority of both drawings and plates the figure style is markedly different from that of other late works by Giovanni Battista in most surviving sketches as well as etchings, it is now necessary to consider this aspect in detail. Although architecture was usually the dominant theme of Piranesi's *vedute* throughout his career, the human figure played a major role in conveying emotional tone and introducing dynamic values into the design. An increasing number of separate figure studies, evidently made from life, which are still coming to light, make it clear that Piranesi, like Watteau, compiled collections of such material for use when the need arose.[56] Unlike the Frenchman's working process, however, few of Piranesi's rapid sketches can be related to specific figures in his plates. Instead, they seem to have suggested ideas that were varied or adapted in the actual process of etching, as has already been mentioned. His early studies and figures of the 1740s represent a wide range of humanity, their wiry and energetic character owing much to Callot, Stefano della Bella, Salvator Rosa and Magnasco. As his *vedute* compositions grew more dramatic from the mid-1750s onwards and his images of Rome assumed a more polemical dimension, his figures were to become more generalised, either existing as minute foils to the superhuman grandeur around them, by means of their gesturing limbs as indicators of salient features, or simply functioning as conductors of directional energy (FIG.5). Gradually, however, towards his final years in the 1770s, this highly-charged vitality was replaced by broader rhythms when he was engaged in recording Hadrian's Villa, Tivoli, among the later etchings for the *Vedute di Roma*.[57] Significantly, in Piranesi's rare surviving compositional drawings for these years, the figures continue to be indicated in a series of scribbled ciphers, thus leaving the final definition to be made by him direct on to the plate. Meanwhile at Pompeii, where he was clearly planning a separate and highly ambitious publication, the figures in the 15 or so surviving drawings (FIG.16) are more precisely defined since, as with Paestum, he began to realise that the final etchings might have to be undertaken by others.[58] Unquestionably drawn by himself, the lines of Piranesi's Pompeian figures become coarser and the figures stiffer in their articulation although losing none of

41

42

their emotive force. According to Hylton Thomas's memorable observation, 'the brevity and power of his strokes recall those qualities in Rembrandt's mature figure drawings. Interior modelling has been concentrated in large patches of intense shadow; contours are heavy and smoother. An indefinable air of brooding melancholy, quite unlike the sharp energy of his earlier figures, deepens the humanity of these figures.'[59]

The comparative detail of the many figures scattered throughout the surviving drawings of Paestum – totalling well over 100 in the 17 compositions concerned – share significant aspects of this late style at Pompeii. However, they still have to be considered as a unique case, given the exceptional circumstances of the Paestum project. Unlike the compositional studies for Tivoli where, despite the possibility of producing a future treatise on Hadrian's Villa, Giovanni Battista was prepared to etch and issue many views individually as part of his *Vedute di Roma*, the Paestum suite was seen as a fully independent project. Work was already sufficiently advanced in the survey and recording stages to merit a set of exceptionally finished drawings. The artist, given his rapidly failing health, had calculated the likelihood of surviving long enough to achieve the major part of the etching process on return to Rome. While such an outstanding student of Piranesi's draughtsmanship as Hylton Thomas has discerned no signs of two hands operating in these drawings, the fact that the figures are varied in quality and inconsistent in scale can be reasonably attributed to the urgency of the exercise.[60] Undoubtedly, practical guidance was needed for the inexperienced Francesco and his father lacked the time to extemporise figures direct on to the plate as he was accustomed to do. (The rejected version of Plate XII (FIG.37) with its uncharacteristic foreground figures, which come far closer to those of the later *Vedute di Roma*, may give an idea of that process if time had allowed it to be carried out on the other plates.) As already mentioned, a substantial proportion of the most prominent figures in the drawings are clearly integrated with the architecture behind them. This is particularly clear in the case of the gesticulating figure in front of the right-hand column in the study for Plate VI where there is a discernible break in the fluting as it meets the body (FIG.23). The fact that certain other drawn figures are superimposed on the pencil outline of the existing architectural composition is of no great significance since this happens regularly in Piranesi's almost contemporary Pompeian drawings (FIG.16) where the figures are relatively defined.

What does become apparent when comparing the drawings and their corresponding plates is the high degree of subtle definition of the architecture in both drawings and etchings, yet the awkwardness and lack of subtlety, both in execution as well as placing, of many of the figures populating the latter, even though the majority of these are already in position (and fully integrated) in the former. In this discrepancy it is plausible to see the less assured hand of Francesco only as etcher, given that we have evidence of his personal figure style in the published Frontispiece (FIG.36), a work not only signed by him but having an additional figure to those shown in the missing

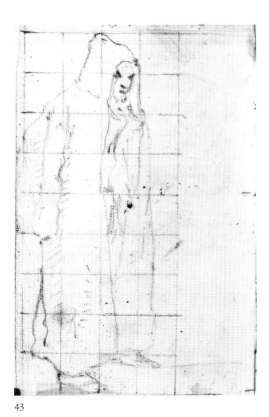

43

44

FIG.43 Giovanni Battista Pirane[
Study for the hooded figure in [
of *Différentes vues de Pesto* …
Pencil (squared for transfer), c. [
(Biblioteca Estense, Modena).

FIG.44 Detail from FIG.30.

preparatory drawing held by his father in the Labruzzi portrait (FRONTISPIECE).
As it happens, some remarkable evidence to confirm Francesco's late and inexpert
intervention in the process has come to light in one of two highly important Piranesi
sketchbooks, discovered in the Biblioteca Estense at Modena during the late 1970s by
Adriano Cavicchi and Silla Zamboni.[61]

   While the first of these albums contains work by Piranesi alone, the second appears
to have been used both by Giovanni Battista as well as his sons during his final years,
as confirmed by some manuscript accounts, dated 7 January 1777, added by Francesco's
younger brother, Angelo (born 1763). In addition to studies for the restored antiquities
published in Giovanni Battista's penultimate publication, *Vasi, Candelabri, Cippi,
Sarcofagi* … (begun earlier but collected in two volumes and published in 1778), the
second sketchbook contains a remarkable series of outline studies in pencil for some
45 figures related to the Paestum plates. These studies possess an assurance and vitality
that can only be ascribed to Giovanni Battista's hand. Their freshness and immediacy
of observation, as well as a sensitivity in the use of the pencil, suggest that Giovanni
Battista intentionally built up an anthology of figures in this album as he prepared the
architectural compositions in which they were to feature as staffage. What is equally

remarkable is that the studies for at least 17 of these figures are squared for transfer; for example that of the watercarrier, minus his donkey (FIG.41), for the preparatory study of Plate XIII (FIG.34, 42) and that of a hooded figure (FIG.43) for the one standing in the centre of the drawing for Plate XVI (FIG.30, 44).[62] Moreover, since most of these drawn figures are substantially larger than their etched counterparts, it seems most likely that the squaring was added by Francesco in the process of reducing them to the scale of the plates where he was ultimately to lack either the finesse or the integrating skills of his father.[63] It hardly needs to be stressed that Giovanni Battista would never have resorted to such an elementary aid in etching his own figures. It seems reasonable to conclude, therefore, that while the surviving compositional drawings in London, Paris and Amsterdam are totally autograph by the father, Francesco's inexpert intervention in the etchings was primarily confined to realising his father's figures.

The legacy of Piranesi and Paestum

James Adam's negative reactions to Paestum in 1761 were by no means untypical of a generation who, while relishing the temples' primitive significance in terms of contemporary taste and theory, found their unfamiliar proportions, comparatively coarse detail and sheer austerity in form of little application to modern design. Significantly, when Soufflot had introduced an engaged version of the Paestum Doric column, with a base and pedestal, into French architecture around 1758, it was to be well out of sight in the crypt of Ste-Geneviève (later the Panthéon), Paris.[64] Even Winckelmann, the High Priest of the Greek Revival who, in his *Remarks on the Architecture of the Ancients* (*Anmerkungen über die Baukunst der Alten*) of 1762, inaccurately claimed to have been among the first to give news of the details of the temples from first-hand contact, made little use of them to support his theories. On the contrary side of the debate, a convinced Roman classicist, such as Chambers (with Major's *Paestum* probably in mind), in 1768–71 could state that: 'In the Constructive Part of Architecture the Antients [sic] were no great Proficients. I believe many of the Deformities which we observe in the Grecian Buildings must be ascribed to their Ignorance in this Particular such as their Gouty Columns … and their Temples with a Range of Columns running in the Center to support the Roof contrary to every Rule both of Beauty and Conveniency ….'[65]

By the end of the previous decade, however, the baseless Doric column had become accepted as an expression of modernity and in 1758 James 'Athenian' Stuart had produced the first ever example in a small temple (based on the Theseum, Athens) at Hagley, Warwickshire, albeit in the modest role of a landscape feature. When the young Soane first visited Paestum with his new-found patron, the mercurial Bishop of Derry, in March 1779 he completed a series of measured sketches, including plans and elevations, comparing them with those given in Major's book. His close study of some of the capitals and entablatures must have required considerable work on ladders. Returning there again in February 1780 with the Bishop and a party of travellers from

Sicily, he noted in his sketchbook that 'The Architecture of the three Temples is Doric but exceeding rude, the temples at the extremities in particular they have all the particulars of the Grecian doric but not the elegance & taste; they seem all formed with the same materials, of stone formed by petrifaction which continues to this day and is found in great abundance between the town and the sea' (FIG.45).'[66] Among the first fruits of these experiences was a design, presented to the Bishop, for an elaborate domed dog kennel, with a triangular plan and featuring the baseless Doric columns Soane had recently studied (FIG.46).[67] Soane also presented the Parma Academy in May 1780 with a drawing of a new Greek Doric version of his triumphal bridge: an unsolicited gift which led to his receiving a diploma of honorary membership.

When compared to the plates of earlier published surveys of Paestum, such as Dumont or Major, the Piranesi etchings of these seminal buildings were to mark a critical watershed between archaeological-polemical concerns and a profound emotional understanding and visual commitment by travellers as much as artists and architects. The impact of Piranesi's plates was beginning to take effect by the time Goethe made his famous initial encounter with the temples in March 1787 – some ten years after Piranesi's expedition and seven after Soane's second visit.[68] Coming from Germany where he had been brought up with the indelible images of the *Vedute di Roma* on his schoolroom walls, he was extremely likely to have seen the Paestum etchings in the artistic circles he frequented in Rome from the time of his arrival there the previous year. Yet even then his reactions, like Soane's, still convey something of the shock of having to abandon long-standing classical preconceptions. As he carefully plots the process of his conversion wrought by the temples he describes how:

> … *at first sight they excited nothing but stupefaction. I found myself in a world which was completely strange to me. In their evolution from austerity to charm, the centuries have simultaneously shaped and created a different man. Our eyes and, through them our whole sensibility have become so conditioned to a more slender style of architecture that these crowded masses of stumpy conical columns appear offensive and even terrifying. But I pulled myself together, remembered the history of art, thought of the age with which this architecture was in harmony, called up images in my mind of the austere style of sculpture – and in less than an hour I found myself reconciled to them and even thanking my guardian angel for having allowed me to see these well-preserved remains with my own eyes.*[69]

By the last decade of the century the use of the Greek Doric entered the design of more sophisticated buildings. In 1789 Joseph Bonomi incorporated four Paestum Doric columns, with powerfully expressed entasis, in corners of the nave of the Earl of Aylesford's estate church at Packington, Warwickshire. For Soane, however, the attraction of such 'primitivism', experienced in Italy and reinforced by Laugier's writings, developed on a more cautious level. For instance, in 1798, as a reminder of

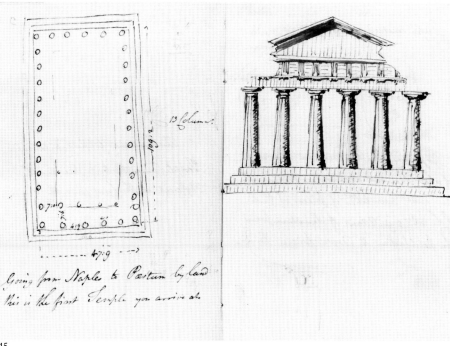

45

their shared experiences, he was to design for his Grand Tour travelling companion
Henry Greswold Lewis a '*Barn à la Paestum*' at Malvern Hall, Warwickshire (FIG.47).
Expressing the utilitarian nature of this structure, he used a series of impressive paired
columns of brick to support a wooden entablature. The following year he was to ele-
vate the Greek Doric to a more sophisticated expression when he employed Joseph
Gandy to incorporate it within a revised version of his prize-winning *Triumphal Bridge*
project, represented by a striking worm's-eye view (FIG.48).[70]

   Moreover, as he entered the new century the order was to be used in Soane's monumental designs with increasing importance. For example a ring of baseless Doric
columns enhanced the solemnity of the interiors of the Bourgeois mausolea, both in
Charlotte Street, London (1807), and at the Dulwich Picture Gallery (1811). At the
Bank of England, pairs of columns *in antis* in the Princes Street Vestibule (1803–8)
referred back to the powerful images of the pronaos of the Temple of Neptune
 and, as he noted in his third Academy lecture of 1810, referring to the use of columns
in the interiors of ancient buildings, 'we have a very singular example of this practice
in one of the temples at Paestum [The Basilica, or Hera I]'.[71] Perhaps the grandest
legacy of Piranesi's Paestum, as seen in Plate x and its related drawing (FIG.27), was
that of the heroic entrance to Soane's projected Mausoleum for the Duke of York in
St James's Park (1827), powerfully rendered in a perspective by Gandy (FIG.49).[72]

46

Soane and the sublime dreams of Piranesi

For all the widespread influence that Piranesi exercised on his formative years and the bold and highly radical forms of classicism developed in his maturity, Soane's public attitude to the great Venetian was expressed in words of censure when appointed Professor of Architecture at the Royal Academy in 1806. Although, along with his friend Turner, he sometimes used Piranesi fantasy compositions as the basis for lecture drawings, his personal predilections conflicted with his public role as educator.[73] Like Reynolds in his Royal Academy *Discourses*, confronted by the idiosyncratic and wayward genius of Gainsborough and Hogarth, Soane experienced considerable tensions between his creative inner vision and the need to construct a coherent, pedagogic system for his students and colleagues. The central problem lay in Piranesi's willingness to push the boundaries of invention to extremes of distortion and complexity in the search for original concepts in design. Soane, with a cautionary attitude, strikingly similar to Chambers's advice on his departure for Italy in 1777, was unbending in his condemnation:

47

48

Facing page
FIG.46 Copy of Soane's 1779 design
for a dog kennel, drawn by Charles
James Richardson, c. 1835. Pencil, pen
and ink with watercolour, 707 × 1272 mm.
(Sir John Soane's Museum).

FIG.47 John Soane. 'Barn à la Paestum',
Solihull, Warwickshire, 1798.

FIG.48 John Soane. Perspective design
for a Triumphal Bridge in the Greek
Doric style, drawn by Joseph Michael
Gandy, 1799. Watercolour, 635 × 970 mm.
(Sir John Soane's Museum).

That men, unacquainted with the remains of Ancient Buildings, should indulge in licentious and whimsical combinations is not a matter of surprise, but that a man, who had passed all his life in the bosom of Classic Art, and in the contemplation of the majestic ruins of Ancient Rome, observing their sublime effects and grand combinations, a man who had given innumerable examples how truly he felt the value of the noble Simplicity of those buildings, that such a man, with such examples before his eyes, should have mistaken Confusion for Intricacy, and undefined lines and forms for Classical variety, is scarcely to be believed; yet such was Piranesi.[74]

Yet ultimately it was within the hermetic world of the house at Lincoln's Inn Fields rather than the public one of the Royal Academy's lecture theatre at Somerset House that Piranesi's far-reaching and potent inspiration for Soane found its true expression. In the 1780s Horace Walpole, in a panegyric to the great Venetian, had recognised the potency of the 'sublime dreams of Piranesi' as an exceptional source

49

FIG.49 John Soane.
Projected Sepulchral Church for the
Duke of York, St James's Park, London,
drawn by Joseph Michael Gandy, 1827.
Watercolour, 810 × 1030 mm.
(Sir John Soane's Museum).

Facing page
FIG.50 Joseph Michael Gandy.
View of the Monument Court,
13 Lincoln's Inn Fields, looking west,
showing the 'Pasticcio'.
Watercolour, 290 × 193 mm.
19th August 1825
(Sir John Soane's Museum).

FIG.51 Joseph Michael Gandy.
View of the Dome area, 13 Lincoln's
Inn Fields, looking east, 1811.
Watercolour, 1370 × 800 mm.
(Sir John Soane's Museum).

of stimulus for contemporary architects.[75] Soane, inspired by the creative thinking
behind the revised plates of Piranesi's experimental prison compositions, the *Carceri
d'Invenzione* (FIG.2), as well as by the Venetian's crowded plates of archaeological
remains, was to create a unique sequence of interiors with complex spatial and structural
ambiguities. Conditioned by mirrors and membranes of clear and coloured glass,
together with the dynamic effects of concealed as well as directed lighting, the spectator
is led through a kaleidoscopic progression of sensations and emotions. Enriching
these effects still further are ingenious encrustations at almost every level and on every
surface of architectural elements, reliefs, sculptures, casts and ornamental features
which, like those in Piranesi's experimental *capricci* (FIG.7) and plates of juxtaposed
fragments, were intended to provide a catalytic effect on the receptive architectural
imagination (FIG.51).[76] As time went on, Soane continued to add to this *mise en scène*
as fresh theatrical effects suggested themselves. For instance, in 1819 he devised a
bizarre Piranesian *capriccio* (or 'Pasticcio' as he called it) in the Monument Court, a
column composed of capitals and other fragments on a Neo-Classical base (FIG.50).
A similar work incorporating the grave of Mrs Soane's dog Fanny, which was erected
in the front courtyard in 1820, was moved to its present location in the Monk's Yard in
1824–5 (FIG.52).[77] The use of features such as the obelisks incorporated into the skyline

View of the Court of the Tivoli Cap: looking Westward,

50

51

of the Monk's Yard is also reminiscent of Piranesi's eclectic compositions, such as found along the walls of his monumental piazza for the Knights of Malta in Rome.[78]

This intensely personal theatre of Soane's creative imagination also served as a form of psychological release in times of stress and anguish. When in the throes of profound disillusionment with his sons' failure to meet his expectations and also deeply hurt by professional censure from the Royal Academy, in 1812 he wrote a profoundly ironic description of his house as if reduced by predatory Time to a mysterious Piranesian ruin (not dissimilar in feeling to Gandy's aerial cut-away perspective of the entire Bank in ruins [FIG. 54], of 1830).[79] This rambling and often incoherent manuscript, entitled *Crude Hints towards an History of my House*, takes the form of an antiquary's conjectures about the origins and functions of the cavernous spaces littered with inscriptions, sculpture and all manner of bewildering debris. Confronted by the absence of a means of communication between various levels and rooms, the imaginary scholar identifies a particular void as having served this function. In his words: 'I am aware it has been supposed that this very space, if a staircase, would only have been one of those Carcerian dark Staircases represented in some of Piranesi's ingenious dreams for prisons.' (FIG.2)[80]

The conceptual journey taken by Piranesi's creative mind from the Palladian rhetoric of the *Bridge of Magnificence*, via the idiosyncratic language of his strangely eclectic mode of design, to the Sublime Primitivism of his images of Paestum, is also reflected in the fertility of Soane's original compositions. Significantly, Soane chose, as a valedictory gesture in 1820, to record the unfettered flights of his own architectural compositions in a sweeping panorama of unrealised projects, disappointed hopes and ideal schemes with a solitary youthful dreamer seated in the foreground. Possessing a Piranesian breadth and mood, this *tour de force* by Joseph Gandy, exhibited at the Royal Academy in 1820, was entitled *Architectural Visions of Early Fancy and Dreams in the Evening of Life* (FIG.53).[81] In its prodigious range this elegiac work comes strikingly close in spirit to the culminating phrase of Thomas de Quincey's contemporary conversation with Coleridge, as reported in *The Confessions of an English Opium Eater*, published a year later, describing the powerful stimulus of Piranesi's imagery in the *Carceri* upon the poet's imagination: 'With the same power of endless growth and self-reproduction did my architecture proceed in dreams.'[82]

FIG.52 View of the Monk's Yard behind No. 14 Lincoln's Inn Fields, looking east showing 'Fanny's Tomb'. Engraving from *A Description of the Residence of Sir John Soane, Architect*, privately printed, 1835.

53

FIG.53 John Soane. *Architectural visions
of early fancy in the gay morning of
youth and dreams in the evening of life*,
drawn by Joseph Michael Gandy, 1820.
Pencil, pen and ink, watercolour
and bodycolour, 735 × 1305 mm.
(Sir John Soane's Museum).

54

FIG.54 John Soane.
Aerial cutaway view of the Bank of
England from the south-east,
drawn by Joseph Michael Gandy, 1830.
Pen and watercolour, 845 × 1400 mm.
(Sir John Soane's Museum).

Author's acknowledgements

In the preparation of this publication I should like to express special thanks to Helen Dorey, Deputy Curator of the Museum, for her constant help and advice, and to Christopher Woodward who first drew my attention to Soane's *Crude Hints* manuscript; to the Director Dr Elisabeth Kieven, and staff of the Bibliotheca Hertziana, Rome, where the text was completed while holding the Rudolf Wittkower Visiting Fellowship; to Professor A.A. Tait; to Professor Silla Zamboni for advice over the critical Piranesi sketchbooks in the Biblioteca Estense, Modena, which he discovered; and to Valerie, Stephen and James who first explored Paestum with me.

Bibliographical abbreviations

Royal Academy, *Soane*
John Soane Architect. Master of Space and Light, exh. cat., ed. M. Richardson and M.A. Stevens, Royal Academy of Arts, 1999.

Watkin, *Soane. Academy Lectures*
David Watkin, *Sir John Soane. Enlightenment Thought and the Royal Academy Lectures*, Cambridge, 1996.

Wilton-Ely, *Piranesi. Complete Etchings*
J. Wilton-Ely, *Giovanni Battista Piranesi. The Complete Etchings*, 2 vols, San Francisco, 1994.

Notes

1 The letter in the Soane Archive (Private Correspondence I.C.7.1) is entitled 'Sir William Chambers to M. Edward Stevens, Architect, Au Caffé Anglois [sic], Place D'Espagna, Rome' and is addressed from Chambers's residence in Berners Street, London, 5 August 1774. The full text is quoted in J. Harris, *Sir William Chambers, Knight of the Polar Star*, London, 1970, pp.21–2.

2 The entire corpus of Piranesi's graphic works is reproduced in J. Wilton-Ely, *Piranesi. Complete Etchings*, while his activities and influence as an architect are considered in J. Wilton-Ely, *Piranesi as Architect and Designer*, New Haven and London, 1993. For a general introduction to his work and career, see J. Scott, *Piranesi*, London and New York, 1976, and J. Wilton-Ely, *The Mind and Art of Piranesi*, London and New York, 1978.

Soane possessed two sets of Piranesi's graphic works: one in 6 volumes, the other in 12. The latter set was bought as late as 3 July 1826 for £24.0.0 from Messers Wood and McCulloch, according to a reference in Soane's Note Book, 1826: 'Paid 24.0.0 for 12 vols Piranesi bound Imperial folio calf entire'. The history of Soane's sets of graphic works, however, is particularly complicated by the fact that he engaged in a series of 'trading-up' exercises in order to improve his holdings. Examples of such acquisition procedures are indicated by the following references: "Agreed with Taylor. Piranesi Works. 50gns, to take my 4 vol and 1 vol Candelabra", Soane Note Book 6 Dec 1793; bought from Thomas Boone 30 May 1817, £2.10.0; "Antonine & Trajan Column" SM Archive 16/12/62; bought from Thomas Boone 9 Sept 1815, £0.7.0, "Antichitata [sic] di Albano", SM Archive 16/12/63; bought from Thomas Boone 16 June 1818, £3.10.0, "Piroli et Piranesi Antiquite d'Herculaneum' 6 vols SM Archive Priv. Corr. XVI.E.3.9.

3 The origins and graphic evolution of the etchings of the *Prima Parte di Architetture e Prospettive* are discussed in detail, along with other seminal fantasies, in A. Robison, *Piranesi. Early Architectural Fantasies. A Catalogue Raisonné of the Etchings*, Chicago and London, 1986. Piranesi's use of the architectural fantasy as medium for personal experiment is examined in J.Wilton-Ely, *Piranesi*, exh. cat., Arts Council of Great Britain, Hayward Gallery, London, 1978, pp.24–6.

4 For the circumstances and genesis of Soane's *Triumphal Bridge*, see Royal Academy, *Soane*, pp.86–95. See also note 70 below. Soane's training and subsequent studies in Italy are discussed in P. de la Ruffinière Du Prey, *John Soane. The Making of an Architect*, Chicago and London, 1982.

5 The complex origins and revisions of the immensely influential *Carceri* plates are discussed and fully illustrated in Robison 1986, op. cit., pp.37–58, 138–210. For a bibliography covering these works, see Wilton-Ely, *Piranesi. Complete Etchings*, I, p.48 and II, appendix. Both Soane's sets of Piranesi's etched works, referred to above, contained the *Carceri* plates in their later and influential state, first issued in 1761. In his strange manuscript fantasy describing his Museum in ruins, *Crude Hints Towards an History of my House*, 1812, Soane was to refer to the striking images of 'those Carcerian dark Staircases represented in some of Piranesi's ingenious dreams for prisons'; see H. Dorey, 'Crude Hints' in *Visions of Ruin. Architectural Fantasies & Designs for Garden Follies*, exh. cat., Sir John Soane's Museum, London, 1999, p.63. See also note 80 below.

6 Piranesi's impact on a wide range of Soane's predecessors and contemporaries, including the Adam brothers, Bélanger, Boullée, Chambers, Clérisseau, Dance the Younger, Desprez, Hope, Ledoux, Robert Mylne and Thomas Sandby is examined in Wilton-Ely, *Piranesi*, exh. cat., 1978, op. cit., *passim*. For Piranesi's impact on Soane's first and 'revered' master, see D. Stroud, *George Dance, Architect, 1741–1825*, London, 1971, p.98.

7 The critical relationship between Robert and James Adam in Rome is examined in J. Fleming, *Robert Adam and his Circle in Edinburgh and Rome*, London, 1962. See also A.A. Tait, *Robert Adam. Drawings and the Imagination*, Cambridge, 1993, *passim*.

8 Fleming 1962, op. cit., p.167. Adam in the same letter goes on to add, with some satisfaction, 'Chambers, who courted Piranesi's friendship with all the assidulty of a lover, never could bring him even to do a sketch of any one thing, and told me I would never be able to get anything from him. So much is he [Chambers] out of his calculation that he [Piranesi] has told me that whatsoever I want of him he will do for me with pleasure, and is just now doing two drawings for me which will be both singular and clever'.

9 The two Piranesi fantasy drawings were acquired on separate occasions by Soane. FIG.3 (Soane Museum: Adam vol.26/163) formed part of an album that was originally purchased by Charles Heathcote Tatham at the Adam sale of 1821 and then bought by Soane in the Tatham sale of 1833. It appears that various items within the album may have been added or rearranged while in

Tatham's possession, but the rebinding of the volume in the early 20th century makes the matter more complex still. FIG.4 (Adam vol.56/146) came from the Adam sale in 1818. FIGS 3 and 4 have always been assumed to be the ones referred to in the Adam letter of 1755, as quoted above in note 8. However, more recently, doubts have been raised over this, owing to the incomplete nature of 26/163 and its markedly different character in style and technique from 56/146, even given that Piranesi's range of draughtsmanship defies any simple evolutionary analysis.

The compositional style and execution of 26/163 (535 × 750 mm), sketched in red chalk and partially defined in brown ink, still possesses much of the delicate and sinuous rococo fantasy of Piranesi's early Roman years of the late 1740s, wherein his Venetian inheritance from the world of Tiepolo was being cross-fertilised with newly encountered inspiration of monumental Roman antiquity. Many of the composition's elaborate architectural features resemble those found in a ruined fantasy plate of the late 1740s, first discovered in 1967 on the backs of two contemporary plates for the *Vedute di Roma*. This latter highly ambitious composition is entitled by Robison 'Fantastic Port Monument' and analysed at length in his *Piranesi. Early Architectural Fantasies*, 1986, op. cit., pp.33–6, 132–3, repr. no.27. Drawing 26/163 is also discussed in D. Stillman, 'Robert Adam and Piranesi' in *Essays in the History of Architecture Presented to Rudolf Wittkower*, ed. D. Fraser, H. Hibberd and M.J. Lewine, London, 1967, pp.198–206; *Soane. Connoisseur & Collector. A Selection of Drawings from Sir John Soane's Collection*, exh. cat., Soane Gallery, London, 1995, no.19.

On the other hand, the composition of drawing 56/146 (385 x 530 mm) with its more vigorously executed techniques and structural monumentality (while strikingly close in theme to the early *Carceri*, of c.1745) appears to belong to the mid-1750s, when Adam first met Piranesi, and is carried out in pen and brown ink and brown wash over a red chalk and slight black chalk sketch. See H. Thomas, *The Drawings of Piranesi*, London, 1954, 46, no.36; see also *Soane. Connoisseur & Collector*, 1995,

op. cit., no.20; A.A. Tait, *Robert Adam. The Creative Mind: from the Sketch to the Finished Drawing*, exh. cat., Soane Gallery, London, 1996, 12, no.6.

10 Soane's introduction to Piranesi could have been facilitated by his master, George Dance the Younger, who was himself in close contact with Piranesi in Rome in 1760 (see 'The Missing Years of Robert Mylne', *Architectural Review*, CXXX, September 1951, pp.179–82). For the complete series of the *Vedute di Roma* and related literature, see Wilton-Ely, *Piranesi. Complete Etchings*, I, pp.176–311; the four given by the artist to Soane being reproduced as follows: *The Pantheon* (no.193), *The Arch of Constantine* (no.230), *The Arch of Septimius Severus* (no.232) and *Tomb of Cecilia Metella* (no.200).

11 In Joseph Gandy's watercolour of 1798 of the Breakfast Room in 12 Lincoln's Inn Fields (SM 14/6/1: Royal Academy, *Soane*, p.158, no.65), where these prints were first recorded on display, it is just possible to discern Piranesi's etchings of the Arches of Constantine (Wilton-Ely, *Piranesi. The Complete Etchings*, no.230) and of Septimius Severus (no.232) hanging high up on the left wall to either side of the interior of S. Maria degli Angeli, Rome (no.262). On the right wall Piranesi's prints of the Pantheon (no.193) and Colosseum (no.191) flank Soane's own Royal Academy silver-medal-winning measured drawing of the Banqueting House, Whitehall. In Soane's own *Description* of his house in 1835 he records that inside the planes on the north side of the Picture Room, above Callcott's painting, *A Passage Point*, were hanging 'four prints of buildings in Rome by Piranesi … presented to me by that great artist.' The earliest inventory of the Museum's contents by the first Curator, George Bailey, in 1836–7, also records: 'These four prints were presented to Sir John Soane by the artist.' The prints are still displayed in the black and gold frames Soane favoured in the 1780s and 1790s. Other Piranesi *vedute* listed among the framed works hanging in the house at Soane's death in 1837 were as follows: in the Picture Room, *The Colosseum* (Wilton-Ely, *Piranesi. The Complete Ecthings* no.191); in the

large bedroom in the attic, *The Exterior of St Peter's* (no.891: this engraving was noted as in extremely poor condition in the late 19th century and has been 'missing' since 1906), *The Interior of S. Maria degli Angeli* (no.262), *The Temple of Vesta at Tivoli* (no.932), *The Tomb of Caius Cestius* (no.884) and *The Exterior of Castel Sant'Angelo* (no.894).

12 For the significance of *Le Antichità Romane*, see J. Wilton-Ely, 'Piranesi and the role of archaeological illustration' in *Piranesi e la Cultura Antiquaria: gli Antecedenti e il Contesto*, ed. A. Lo Bianco, Università degli Studi di Roma, Rome, 1983, pp.317–38. The impact of Piranesi's didactic techniques of illustration on Soane's specialised progress and construction views as well as in his Academy lecture drawings was extensive. For examples of the former, see *Buildings in Progress. Soane's Views of Construction*, exh. cat., Soane Gallery, 1995.

13 Gandy's pen and watercolour painting of the Rotunda and Four and Five Per cent Offices at the Bank of England in ruins (SM P127), painted in 1798, was exhibited at the Royal Academy in 1832 under the title '*Architectural ruins: a vision*'. See Royal Academy, *Soane*, p.231 (no.133).

14 According to Adam, writing in a letter of April 1756: 'in one of the frontispieces representing the Appian Way in all its ancient splendour, with all the mausoleums of the Consuls, Emperors &ca [sic], he [Piranesi] has taken the occasion to put in [Allan] Ramsay's name and mine, with our Elogiums, as if buried in these tombs' (Fleming 1962, op. cit., p.207). The monument inscribed to Adam is placed beneath the sculptural group of *Romulus and Remus with She Wolf* to the left of the composition while Ramsay's less impressive one is among the tombs flanking the Via Appia. A similar fantasy of the Circus Maximus, used by Piranesi as frontispiece to the other volume of the *Antichità* devoted to funerary monuments, provided the basis of one of Soane's lecture illustrations (SM 20/4/4), as reproduced in *Soane and Death*, ed. G. Waterfield, exh. cat., Dulwich Picture Gallery, 1996, p.12, fig.2.

15 Piranesi's intellectual and artistic responses to

the Graeco-Roman controversy are discussed in J. Wilton-Ely, 'Vision and Design. Piranesi's "fantasia" and the Graeco-Roman controversy' in *Piranèse et les Français. Actes du Colloque tenu à la Villa Médicis* (1976), ed. G. Brunel, Académie de France à Rome, Rome, 1978, pp.529–52.

16 The full text and illustrations of *Della Magnificenza*, of considerable importance to Soane in theoretical as well as practical terms, are reproduced in *G.B. Piranesi. The Polemical Works*, ed. J. Wilton-Ely, Farnborough, 1972. Piranesi's reciprocal relationship with Adam in the production of the *Campo Marzio*, and the remarkable character of the book, are examined in J. Wilton-Ely, 'Utopia or Megalopolis? The "Ichnographia" of Piranesi's "Campus Martius" reconsidered' in *Piranesi fra Venezia e l'Europa*, ed. A. Bettagno, Florence, 1983, pp.293–304. The giant fantasy plan (*Ichnographia*) of the Campus Martius area of Rome, devised by Piranesi as a conscious anthology of ingenious planning forms, is shown to have influenced Soane's projected mausoleum for James King (1777) in M. McCarthy, 'Thomas Pitt, Piranesi and John Soane. English architects in Italy in the 1770s', *Apollo*, XXXIV (December 1991), pp.380–86.

17 For the full text and etched polemical fantasy compositions, with discussion of their impact on contemporary design, see G.B. Piranesi, *Observations on the letter of Monsieur Mariette with Opinions on Architecture, and a Preface to a New Treatise on the Introduction and Progress of the Fine arts in Europe in Ancient Times*. Introduction by John Wilton-Ely. Translation by Caroline Beamish and David Britt. Getty Research Institute, Los Angeles, 2002.

18 Piranesi's two principal architectural commissions for the Rezzonico pope and cardinal G.B. Rezzonico at the Lateran and S. Maria del Priorato, respectively, are discussed in Wilton-Ely 1993, op. cit., while the main preparatory designs are also analysed and reproduced in *Piranesi Architetto*, ed. J. Connors and J. Wilton-Ely, exh. cat., American Academy, Rome, 1992.

19 For a detailed account of the history and design of Piranesi's buildings on the Aventine hill for the Knights of Malta, see Wilton-Ely 1993, op. cit.,

pp.87–119. See also Wilton-Ely, 'Piranesi architetto' and related entries in *Piranesi e l'Aventino*, ed. B. Jatta, exh. cat., Sovrano Ordine Militare di Malta & Biblioteca Apostolica Vaticano [S. Maria del Priorato], Rome, 1998, pp.63–78, nos 172–84. The drawing of the elevation and plan for Piranesi's façade of S. Maria del Priorato (SM Adam vol.27/48) (FIG.8) is executed in pen and ink (304 × 190 mm) in an unidentifiable hand. It has particular value as being the only surviving detailed record of the building, as executed in 1764–5, before the attic storey was destroyed by French artillery in the Risorgimento siege of Rome in 1849.

The second drawing, which records in partial detail the elevation of the high altar of S. Maria del Priorato as carried out (SM Adam vol.26/177) (FIG.9), is also executed in pen and black/brown inks (307 × 193 mm) and is inscribed at the top 'upon the globe is placed a saint' (referring to the omission of the full sculptural composition of the *Apotheosis of St Basil of Cappadocia* in the completed work). This drawing, in the hand of a similar copyist to the other two, may also have been taken from a late stage in design since there are minor differences in the position of the left-hand putto in the figurative detail. In terms of the evolution in design, this work seems to fall between two surviving elevational drawings by Piranesi in the Kunstbibliothek, Berlin, and the Pierpont Morgan Library, New York, respectively (reproduced in Wilton-Ely 1993, op. cit., 107, fig.103 and plate 3).

Lastly, the elevation for the entrance screen to the Piazza de' Cavalieri di Malta (SM Adam vol.26/178) [FIG.10], in pen and brown ink with grey wash (121 x 270 mm), is inscribed 'the West side' in a similar hand and significantly shows some minor differences between the executed building and the only surviving preliminary design by Piranesi, represented by a sketch elevation in the Kunstbibliothek, Berlin (reproduced in Wilton-Ely 1993, op. cit., 92, fig.86). While all the ornamental reliefs are depicted as executed, the Soane drawing shows an apron panel immediately below each of the four windows, as shown in the Berlin design but omitted in the final work.

These three drawings, which belonged to James Adam, may have come into his possession while he was in Rome after his brother, between 1761 and 1763, and in regular contact with Piranesi who was then in the preliminary stages of the Aventine commission. See Fleming 1962, op. cit., *passim*. Volume 27, in which the first drawing was inserted, was acquired by Soane along with the other Adam drawings in 1833 and did not come direct from an Adam sale.

20 For the general influence of Piranesi's etched designs in the *Diverse Maniere*, see Wilton-Ely 1993, op. cit., *passim*; on Soane in particular, see Watkin, *Soane. Academy Lectures*, pp.60–62, 263. Robin Middleton, in his essay, 'Soane's spaces and the matter of fragmentation' (in Royal Academy, *Soane*, pp.34–5), among various influences, suggests the possible impact of one of Piranesi's two plates of his painted wall scheme in the Egyptian manner (now disappeared) in the Caffè degli Inglesi, Rome (Wilton-Ely, *Piranesi. Complete Etchings*, II, no.875), on Soane's positioning of Thomas Banks's sculpture of 'Camadeva and the crocodile' on the east Library bookcase in Lincoln's Inn Fields.

21 For the full repertoire of Piranesi's restored antiquities, depicted in the *Vasi, Candelabri, Cippi, Sarcofagi …*, and the collectors involved, see Wilton-Ely, *Piranesi. Complete Etchings*, II, pp.961–1089.

22 At least four antiquities etched by Piranesi, either from his own collection or known to him, were acquired by Soane in a variety of ways and are evaluated in Professor Cornelius Vermeule's unpublished *Catalogue of Classical Antiquities in Sir John Soane's Museum* (limited typescript edition produced by the author 1975). The rectangular cinerary urn illustrated in FIG.11 (Soane no.M429; Vermeule 323) was one of five illustrated in a composite plate of the *Vasi, Candelabri, Cippi, Sarcofagi …* (Wilton-Ely, *Piranesi. Complete Etchings*, II, no.892). According to Piranesi's caption, this particular work ('B') was found in a tomb near Siena and bought by the celebrated restorer Bartolomeo Cavaceppi (Vermeule considered the base and, probably, the lid to be modern) before entering an English collection.

Soane acquired it from Lord Bessborough's sale in 1802.

Among works from Piranesi's own collection was a heavily restored urn with mourning genii with reversed torches (Soane M726; Vermeule 340) on the east side of the Dome. This object, without lid or base, was etched by Piranesi in another multiple image in the *Vasi* (Wilton-Ely, II, no.915) and was purchased at Lord Mendip's sale in 1802.

In the colonnade leading from the Picture Room to the Dome is a marble capital featuring confronted dolphins (Soane M565; Vermeule 63) which Piranesi illustrated in his polemical defence of Roman originality, *Della Magnificenza ed Architettura de' Romani* (1761), Plate XIX (Wilton-Ely, II, no.779). According to the caption of this large fold-out plate, capital no.4 was found 'In vinea Borioni ad Portam Salariam'. This work was one of the Tatham-Holland marbles, which were collected in and around Rome by Charles Heathcote Tatham for the architect Henry Holland, and was acquired by Soane after the latter's death, probably from his nephew Henry Rowles. Tatham's copies of his letters to Holland during this period, together with the accompanying drawings, were also to be acquired by Soane. In support of this Piranesian provenance, the author is indebted to Dr Ruth Guilding for drawing his attention to one letter in particular in which Tatham describes the fragments in Piranesi's studio which Canova helped him to acquire, as being from his 'museo' (Tatham letters: SM, AL5D 10 July 1795, p.80).

The fragmentary Egyptian capital of limestone (Soane M76; Vermeule 35), of a Ptolemaic style datable to c.150BC, is illustrated by Piranesi among six other fragments in his *Trofei di Ottaviano Augusto*, 1753, pl.II (Wilton-Ely, I, no.274) as 'giacente vicino all'arco de' Pantani' ['found in the vicinity of the Arch of the Pantani']. The Egyptian capital was acquired at the Adam sale of 1818, forming Lot 92 'Part of a capital in Egyptian taste, very curious'. Soane purchased it for £2.2.0., and it was marked down to him, both in his own copy of the sale catalogue and that in the Christie's archive.

Subsequent to Professor Vermeule's work,

Dr Glenys Davies of the Department of Classics, Edinburgh University, who has made a study of techniques used in Piranesi's workshop, has identified the four rectangular marble cinerary urns, M373, M404, M424 and M708, as possibly coming also from this source. In such cases the lids were often transferred from other such objects while new bases were provided by the restorers. For an account of the world of dealing and the restoration of classical antiquities in which Piranesi operated, see S. Howard, 'An antiquarian handlist and the beginnings of the Pio Clementino' in *Antiquity Restored. Essays on the Afterlife of the Antique*, Vienna, 1990, pp.142–53. An early appreciation of the significance of Soane's collection of antiquities, as well as the significance of Piranesi's archaeological etchings, is to be found in A. Michaelis, *Ancient Marbles of Great Britain*, trans. C.A. M. Fennell, 2 vols, Cambridge, 1882. For the most recent research on Soane's collection and display of antiquities, see the unpublished Ph.D. thesis by Ruth Guilding, *Classical Sculpture and the English Interior, 1640–1840. Purpose and Meaning*, University of Bristol, 2000.

23 See M. McCarthy, 'Documents on the Greek Revival in architecture', *Burlington Magazine*, CXIV (November 1972), p.766; Royal Academy, *Soane*, p.110, no.34, repr. A cork model of the Temple of Neptune in the Soane Museum (illustrated in McCarthy's article in figs 39 and 40), which is quite distinct from the three cork models of the Paestum temples, on a larger scale, by Domenico Padiglione, is tentatively attributed by Professor McCarthy to Rosa. Unlike the later works, which show the temple interiors relatively cleaned up, the former model represents the jumbled heaps of fallen masonry and rough vegetation within the cella, as if attempting to translate Piranesi's drawings into a three-dimensional form. See also note 36 below.

24 For a summary of the circumstances behind Piranesi's book on Paestum and for reproductions of all the etched plates, see Wilton-Ely, *Piranesi. Complete Etchings*, II, pp.777–800. Among particularly important studies on the subject are R. Pane, 'Piranesi at Paestum' in *Piranesi fra Venezia e l'Europa*, op. cit., pp.377–88; Pane, *Paestum nelle*

Acqueforti di Piranesi, Milan, 1980.

25 The posthumous portrait of Piranesi by Pietro Labruzzi (1739–1805) is signed 'Labruzzi fece 1779' and shows the study for the frontispiece to the Paestum volume in the sitter's hand as inscribed 'Veduta di tre Tempi Antichi/esistenti nella citta di Possidonia/detta oggi Pesto nel regno di Napoli/opera ultima del Cav. Giov. Bat. Piranesi/1778'. For its relationship to Nollekens's bust of the artist, *circa* 1760, see J. Wilton-Ely, 'A bust of Piranesi by Nollekens', *Burlington Magazine*, CXVIII (August 1976), pp.593–5. See also *Piranesi e l'Aventino*, ed. B. Jatta, 1998, op. cit., p.193, no.50.

26 The funerary candelabrum (partly shown in the right background of the Labruzzi portrait) was initially placed over Piranesi's tomb in S. Maria del Priorato and is now in the Louvre. Its history and function, as well as that of the artist's two prints of it included among the *Vasi* plates, are discussed in *Piranesi e l'Aventino*, ed. B. Jatta, 1998, op. cit., pp.188–9, nos 46a and b.

27 For the context of Paestum in the intellectual background and early history of the Greek Revival, see N. Pevsner and S. Lang, 'The Doric Revival' in Pevsner, *Studies in Art, Architecture and Design*, London, 1968, II, pp.197–211; D. Wiebenson, *Sources of Greek Revival Architecture*, London, 1969; J.M. Crook, *The Greek Revival. Neo-Classical Attitudes in British Architecture. 1760–1970*, London, 1972; R. Middleton and D. Watkin, *Neo-Classical and 19th Century Architecture*, I, London, 1980.

28 W. Herrmann, *Laugier and Eighteenth Century French Theory*, London, 1962; see also a translation, with introduction, of Laugier's *Essai sur l'architecture* by Wolfgang and Anni Herrmann, Los Angeles, 1977. Soane was to use a lecture drawing (SM 23/4/8) based on one of Piranesi's plates refuting Laugier's theories in *Della Magnificenza ed Architettura de' Romani*, 1761, pl.XXVII, reproduced in Royal Academy, *Soane*, p.119, no.41.

29 For a discussion of the three Doric temples at Paestum according to recent excavations, see A.W. Lawrence and R.A. Tomlinson, *Greek Architecture*, Harmondsworth, 1983, revised edition, pp.156–9, 181–4, which also covers the main surviving Greek temples in Sicily. See also P.C. Sestieri, *Paestum*, Rome, 1960, which has

been largely superseded by the most recently available site publication, L. Rota and C.A. Fiammenghi, *Paestum*, Milan, 1984. A detailed photographic record of the site is provided in M. Napoli, *Paestum*, Novara, 1970.

30 The rediscovery and early publications of Paestum are listed and examined in S. Lang, 'The early publications of the temples at Paestum', *Journal of the Warburg and Courtauld Institutes*, XIII (1950), pp.48–64. See also Wiebenson 1969, op. cit., *passim*. For a substantial reassessment with new evidence and abundant documentation, see J.R. Serra (ed.), *La Fortuna di Paestum e la Memoria Moderna del Dorico*, exh. cat. [Certosa di S. Lorenzo a Padula, Salerno], 2 vols, Florence, 1986; Serra, *La Fortuna di Paestum e la Memoria del Dorico, 1750–1830*, exh. cat. [Palazzo Braschi, Rome] and Serra, *Paestum and the Doric Revival, 1750–1830*, exh. cat. [National Academy of Design, New York], Florence, 1986. A particularly valuable anthology of early accounts and images is provided in Serra (ed.), *Paestum. Idea e Immagine*, Modena, 1990.

31 Recent research has established that among the earliest evidence of knowledge about the temples' existence, if not their significance, is the plan of the Paestum area in Costantino Gatta's *Memorie Topografiche-Storiche della Provincia di Lucania …*, Naples, 1732, p.263; see Serra [Florence, 1986], op. cit., I, p.28. Apart from the English traveller Robert Smith's curiosity in making drawings of the temples in 1733, it was the architect Mario Gioffredo's far greater perception when seeing them in 1746 that led to Gazzola's critical pioneering survey; op. cit., pp.27–9.

32 As quoted from a transcription of North's full account in a letter to Charles Dampier of September 1753, in the Warwickshire County Record Office, first published in McCarthy 1972, op. cit., pp.760–61; also reproduced in full with comments in Serra 1990, op. cit., pp.28–9.

33 The painted view of Paestum by Antonio Joli (*circa* 1700–1777), among the earliest documented of the site, is one of a series of *vedute* of Naples and area commissioned by John, Lord Brudenell, later Marquess of Monthermer, during his Grand Tour stay in the city between 1756 and 1768. See

Grand Tour. The Lure of Italy in the Eighteenth Century, ed. A. Wilton and I. Bignamini, exh. cat., Tate Gallery, London, 1996, p.235, no.184.

34 Fleming 1962, op. cit., p.293. Interestingly, Laugier in 1769 came to similar conclusions from publications on buildings in Greece and Southern Italy, stating that: 'in the ruins of Greece there is not one profile or one interesting architectural detail of which one could hope to make successful use in practice'. Quoted in Herrmann 1962, op. cit., p.23.

35 Soane bought a folio of Major's drawings for his key publication, *The Ruins of Paestum*, in 1800. See Royal Academy, *Soane*, p.98, fig.105. For the background to Major's work on Paestum, the original drawings acquired by Soane and particularly their context in relation to other British studies of the site, see M. McCarthy, 'New light on Thomas Major's "Paestum" and later English drawings of Paestum' in Serra 1986, op. cit., pp.47–55.

36 The cork model of the Temple of Neptune is one of three made by Domenico Padiglione (*fl.* 1802–30) of the Greek temples at Paestum and, according to the original Museum inventories, acquired from the collection of Soane's pupil, John Sanders, around 1826. They were probably made in the early 1800s, post-dating the first excavations and restorations (begun in 1802) when a quantity of accumulated fragments were removed from within each building. An earlier cork model of the Temple of Neptune in the Museum, which shows the state of the cella interior before these early restorations, has been attributed by Professor McCarthy to Augusto Rosa, and dated *circa* 1777, see McCarthy 1972, op. cit., p.766; Royal Academy, *Soane*, p.110, no.34, repr. See also note 23 above.

37 Legrand, one of Piranesi's earliest biographers, who was in close contact with the artist's children, left behind a manuscript life of the artist, now in the Bibliothèque Nationale, Paris: *Notice historique sur la vie et les ouvrages de J.B. Piranesi … Rédigée sur les notes et les pièces communiquées par ses fils, les Compagnons et les Continuateurs de ses nombreux travaux* [1799], transcribed in G. Erouart and M. Mosser, 'A propos de la "Notice historique sur la vie et les ouvrages de J.-B. Piranesi": origine

et fortune d'une biographie' in *Piranèse et les Français*, ed. Brunel, 1978, op. cit., pp.213–52. According to Legrand on the origin of Piranesi's attraction to Paestum: 'Quelques artistes ayant rapporté des dessins de ces trois monumens si imposans de Paestum ou Posidonia dans la grande Grèce faisant aujourd'hui partie du Royaume de Naples, Piranesi ne résista point au désir d'aller examiner ces superbes débris: il partit avec son fils et son ami Benedetto Mori, visita e mesura les ruines d'Herculanum [*sic*] et de Pompéia dont ils ne pouvaient s'arracher; en arrivant au pied des Temples de Paestum il fut si frappé du caractère de leur architecture qu'il ne se lassait pas de les admirer de les dessiner sur tous les points. Il eût voulu pour n'échapper aucun détail pouvoir les rendre aussi grands que la nature. Ce désir est exprimé dans ces planches qui donnent une bien juste idée de l'imposant effet de ses masses gigantesques, que les proportions les plus mâles aggrandissent encore à l'oeil' (p.247). Inevitably, following the famous expedition of de Marigny to Paestum in 1750, drawings of the temples were in circulation at the French Academy as well as also among the British circle of designers in Rome. Among the latter, Robert Mylne had gone as far as Agrigento in Sicily in 1757 to make drawings of the Greek temple of Concord, used by Winckelmann in his principal work on architecture, *Anmerkungen überdie Baukunst der alten Tempel zu Girgenti in Sizilien* (1759) and later by Piranesi in *Della Magnificenza* (1761). Mylne also appears to have made drawings at Paestum as used by Thomas Major for his book on the temples. For the latter, see note 35.

38 See Serra 1990, op. cit., p.84. According to Piranesi's caption to the frontispiece, affirming the significance of the Italian location for the temples' design: 'Les voyageurs connoisseurs assurent, que par rapport à l'Architecture Grecque des Temples Bâtis dans l'Ordre Dorique, ceux de Pesto, sont supérieurs en beauté à ceux, qu'on voit en Sicilie et dans la Grèce, et que sans se donner la peine, et la fatigue de longs voyages, ceux ci peuvent suffire pour contenter la curiosité, et qu'enfin cette grande, et majesteuse Architecture donné en son genre l'idée la plus parfait de ce bel

Art.' According to the caption to plate XII involving the Temple of Neptune, the flexibility of the ancient designer's attitude to rules is expressed as follows: 'Cette ouvrage montre bien que l'architecte étoit, mâitre de son art qu'il n'étoit point retenu par des Systéme imaginés capricieusement, ou même dependents de l'imitation des ouvrages en bois; et en placent les trigliphes L dans un tel lieu, il a fait voir que c'étoit un ornement capricieux qui ne dépendoit pas les Loix, ni de principes fondés en raison; mais par les motifs qui ont été allégués dans la planche x.'

39 When the Soane drawings were removed from their frames by the Museum's paper conservator, Mrs Margaret Schuelein, in 1987, a number were found to have significant inscriptions on the versos referring to their use in Soane's lectures (see note 48 below). Given this opportunity to measure the 15 individual sheets, their comparative dimensions to the etched area of the relevant plates (bearing in mind that the former's dimensions are approximate since the sheets are irregular in shape) are as follows (drawing precedes etching, height precedes width in millimetres): Pl.II: 455 × 673/ 437 × 667; Pl.III: 500 × 660/494 × 668; Pl.IV: 461 × 663/468 × 670: Pl.V: 690 × 675/488 × 668; Pl.VI: 460 × 661/466 × 706; Pl.VII: 455 × 672/ 454 × 667; Pl.VIII: 475 × 677/483 × 656; Pl.IX: 686 × 670/466 × 664; Pl.X: 502 × 693/476 × 706; Pl.XI: 450 × 662/448 × 667; Pl.XII: 450 × 682/ 445 × 675; Pl.XIII: 484 × 687/495 × 678; Pl.XIV: 472 × 665/465 × 660; Pl.XVI: 476 × 666/495 × 674; Pl.XVII: 456 × 673/ 446 × 668.

For the relative drawing/etching dimensions of the other surviving drawings in Paris and Amsterdam, see notes 45 and 47 respectively.

40 In the drawing for Plate IX (FIG.26) it is possible to see an early stage of these compositions where the perspectival and architectural structures are resolved and the main figure studies in the foreground worked out in detail. Details of surface texture and stronger effects of light are yet to be added, along with clouds and enlivening foliage. Later still would be added in many cases the alphabetical letters relating to the captions below (see, for example, the drawing for Plate VII, in FIG.25). For illustrations of Piranesi's comparatively few surviving compositional studies, before the

Pompeii and Paestum years, largely outlining the perspectival system concerned, see Wilton-Ely, The Mind and Art of Piranesi, 1978, op. cit., pp.35 (fig.36), 38 (figs 52–3), 42 (fig.60) and 43 (fig.62).

41 Legrand, 'Notice historique' in Erouart & Mosser 1978, op. cit., p.231.

42 Thomas 1954, op. cit, p.31.

43 Legrand, 'Notice historique' in Erouart & Mosser 1978, op. cit., p.232.

44 The kind of spatial experiences evoked by Piranesi's 'scenographic' view-points is borne out by Goethe's comments following his visit to Paestum in 1787. (By then he is likely already to have seen Piranesi's plates.) Recalling his visit to the temples he wrote: 'only when one moves around them, through them, does one really communicate life to them; one feels the life out of them again that the architect intended, yes, that he created into them' (as quoted in Watkin, Soane. Academy Lectures, p.201, from the translation of the Italienische Reise, ed. E. Trunz, Munich, 1989, p.220). Similarly Soane, in comparing Vanbrugh's Blenheim to Paestum in his Royal Academy Lecture IX (1815), observes: 'there is a constant variety of outline that pleases from whatever point it is viewed (as are viewed ancient temples), whether at a distance wherein the great masses only are made out, or at a nearer approach when the prominent features are distinguished, or still nearer where the general details are distinguished. Here the eye reposes to enjoy the whole picture … In this respect the interest is kept up as in the ancient temples, but this would not be the case if variety of outline and continuity of character were confined to one front only. To keep up the first impression there must be the same character observed in every part externally and internally. This is seen in the great temple [i.e. Neptune] at Paestum. Its interior is of the same character as the exterior' (op. cit., pp.372–3).

45 For the Bibliothèque Nationale study for Plate I (Cabinet des estampes, Bd.11 réserve, p.8), see FIG.17; also Thomas 1954, op. cit., pp.55–6, no.58; also Piranesi. Disegni, ed. A. Bettagno, exh. cat., Fondazione Cini, Venice, 1978, p.71, no.85. Executed in pen and brown ink with wash over traces of pencil, its overall dimensions are 480 × 693 mm,

as opposed to those of the etched plate of 439 × 668 mm.

46 Earlier examples of Piranesi's deliberate exclusion of an existing colonnade to allow a more informative view can be seen in the cut-away views of the interior of S. Paolo fuori delle Mura and the porch of the Pantheon in the Vedute di Roma (Wilton-Ely, Piranesi. The Complete Etchings, I, nos 138 and 215 respectively).

47 For the Rijksmuseum study for Plate XIX (1960: 205; I 9972), see FIG.18; also Piranesi. Disegni, ed. Bettagno, 1978, op. cit., p.70, no.84. Executed like the Soane compositions in pen and ink with sepia wash over traces of sanguine and pencil, its overall dimensions are 465 × 675 mm, as opposed to those of the etched plate of 462 × 660 mm.

48 The Paestum drawings are in the type of frames used by Soane for his architectural watercolours in the 1820s; namely wide, flat and with a curved bevel at inner and outer edge. Before Soane framed them it appears that some were used to illustrate his Royal Academy lectures. When the drawings were temporarily removed from their original frames for conservation in 1987 (see note 39), certain drawings were found to be inscribed in pencil on the back as follows: (P69) 7 lecture, No.21 1819/7 lecture 1820; (P72) 1819; (P74) 1820; (P75) 1819; (P139) 5 lecture 1819; (P146) 7 Lecture 1820. Moreover, inside the frame of P139 were strips of early 19th-century paper, one signed John Soane Oct 16th 1805, and another strip from a Soane pamphlet relating to the Law Courts of 1820s. The date 1805, however, is unlikely to have great significance as the drawing in question remained unframed in 1819, judging by the inscription on the same verso. In conclusion, it would seem that the drawings were at least in Soane's possession by 1819. The fact that the drawings appear not to have been used in Soane's lectures as originally given from 1809 onwards (he used others to illustrate Paestum) and appear only for the first time in 1819, helps to establish this fact.

A drawing now at Winterthur dated 6 August 1820 shows an arrangement of Piranesi works in the front bedroom on the second floor of 13 Lincoln's Inn Fields. It shows six Piranesi works above the fireplace and the veduta of Castel

Sant'Angelo and a 'small Piranesi' on the opposite wall. It cannot be certain that those on the fireplace wall are some of the Paestum drawings but the uniform flat frames seem to suggest this. The Paestum drawings could only have been transferred to the Picture Room, where they were distributed singly among other framed works during Soane's lifetime, after its construction in 1824. In 1984–5 Peter Thornton grouped all 15 of them together behind the hinged planes on the north side of the Picture Room to protect them from light.

49 For the unique proof pull of discarded plate XII with blank cartouche (omitted in the replaced plate), see FIG.37; also A. M. Hind, *Giovanni Battista Piranesi. A Critical Study with a List of his Published Works and Detailed Catalogues of the Prisons and the Views of Rome*, London, 1922 (reprinted 1978), p.87, plate LXXIV. While not appearing in any of the preparatory drawings, cartouches containing the captions appear within 10 of the 20 published plates. Proof pulls of Paestum plates with blank captions for plates III and IX, in the collection of the National Gallery of Art, Washington, are illustrated in *The Eye of Thomas Jefferson*, ed. W.H. Adams, exh. cat., Washington, DC, 1976, p.87 (entries by Andrew Robison), figs 139–40. Another proof impression of this rejected version of plate XII (formerly from the collection of the Victorian painter William Bell Scott), which appeared on the art market in 1972, shows evidence of later work than found in the British Museum one. Apart from a general strengthening of the lines, the reworking includes birds in the sky, clouds more clearly defined by intervening etched parallels, and the square top of the extreme left capital, or 'abacus', appears to obtrude on the left far less underneath the hanging fronds by several millimetres. While the British Museum proof is somewhat grey and bland, the later impression is much darkened overall and conveys a general fattening of the forms.

50 Scott 1975, op. cit., p.319.

51 A discussion of the relationship and respective works of father and son is provided in *Giovanni Battista e Francesco Piranesi*, ed. M. Calvesi, exh. cat., Calcografia Nazionale, Rome, 1967; a show

held as a result of the presence of almost all of Piranesi's original copperplates, including those for the frontispiece and all 20 views of Paestum, in the Calcografia where they have been since 1839. A summary of the diverse opinions of scholars on the respective contributions of father and son to the Paestum plates is given in A. Cavicchi and S. Zamboni, 'Due "taccuini" inediti di Piranesi', in *Piranesi tra Venezia e l'Europa*, ed. Bettagno, 1983, op. cit., pp.215–16, note 49. See also note 61 below.

52 Despite the three plates actually signed by Francesco (Frontispiece and Plates XIX and XX), according to Legrand, Giovanni Battista 'grava lui-même dix-neuf de ces planches dont la totalité s'élève à vingt et un, les deux autres furent achevées par son fils Francois Piranesi qui termina également plusieurs autres ouvrages …' ('Notice historique', in Erouart & Mosser 1978, op. cit., p.247).

53 As mentioned previously (see note 25), in the posthumous Labruzzi portrait of Giovanni Battista (FRONTISPIECE), which was produced shortly after his death, the artist holds what seems certain to be the missing compositional drawing for the Paestum frontispiece. In the portion visible, the partially shown inscription is significantly not only in Italian, as opposed to the French version of the plate signed by Francesco (FIG.36), but finishes with the phrase '[ope]ra Ultima del Cav. Gio. Bat. Piranesi/ 1778'. Moreover, at least one figure added by Francesco in front of the inscribed stone in the etched plate (FIG.39) is missing in the represented drawing. The shape of the stone, in any case, is changed in the plate and the figure smoking a pipe is brought to the right-hand edge to reveal an improbably long leg.

54 Legrand, 'Notice historique', in Erouart & Mosser 1978, op. cit., p.247.

55 Francesco Piranesi's frontispiece study in the Kunstbibliothek, Berlin (N.I. 6299/30015) (FIG.40), acquired in 1942, bears the inscription: 'Ferdinando IV/ Regi-Utriusque-Siciliae/Literarum-Artium-Q-Antiuarum/ Restitutori-Munificentissimo/ Monumenta-Paestana/Franciscus-Piranesius'. According to an alphabetical key at the bottom left, it suggests that Francesco intended to include

in this proposed work his father's Paestum plates (a portion of the Temple of Neptune appears to the right) along with fresh plates of such sites as the Grotto of the Sibyl at Cumae and finds from Herculaneum in the museum at Portici. See also *Italienische Zeichnungen der Kunstbibliotek Berlin. Architectur und Dekoration 18. bis 18. Jahrhundert*, ed. S. Jacob, Berlin, 1975, p.177, no.901.

56 Giovanni Battista Piranesi's changing figure styles and functions are examined in Thomas 1954, op. cit., pp.25–7, 59–62; R. Bacou, 'A propos des dessins de figures de Piranèse' in *Piranèse et les Français*, ed. Brunel, 1978, op. cit., pp.33–42.

57 Almost all of Piranesi's etchings and preparatory drawings of the Villa Adriana, many of which are close in date to those of Paestum, are reproduced and discussed in W.L. Macdonald and J.A. Pinto, *Hadrian's Villa and its Legacy*, New Haven and London, 1995, pp. 158, 246–65; see also Thomas 1954, op. cit., pp.21–2.

58 Piranesi's drawings of Pompeii are evaluated in H. Thomas, 'Piranesi and Pompeii', *Kunstmuseets Arsskrift*, Copenhagen, 1956, pp.13–28. Since Thomas's pioneering article a considerable number of other drawings have come to light and seven are discussed and reproduced in *Piranesi. Disegni*, ed. Bettagno, 1978, op. cit., pp.66–70, nos 78–83.

59 Thomas 1954, op. cit., p.27.

60 According to Thomas, 'It is impossible for me to see more than one hand in these drawings. The figures show the same technique as the rest of the drawing, in many cases … appearing in varying stages of completion, exactly in the way the architecture does. Stylistically there is no difference between figures and architecture. The figures are more placid and less dramatic than the ones peopling the Roman views, but they agree perfectly in mood with the subject – all the Paestum scenes exude a tranquillity approaching pastoral somnolence' (op. cit., p.56).

61 A. Cavicchi and S Zamboni, 'Due "taccuini" inediti di Piranesi', in *Piranesi tra Venezia e l'Europa*, ed. Bettagno, 1983, op. cit., pp.177–216. See also Zamboni, 'Due quaderni di Piranesi scoperti nella Biblioteca Estense di Modena', *Studi Romani, Rivista Trimestrale dell'Istituto di Studi Romani*,

Rome, XXVII, n.3 (July–September 1979), pp.332–4. The two sketchbooks in the Biblioteca Estense, Modena, were discovered among the considerable papers of the collector and historian Marchese Giuseppe Campori (1821–1887) which were acquired by the library in 1839. The presence of the notebooks may be connected with a group of more than a hundred autograph letters between Francesco Piranesi and a Swedish correspondent, Don Lorenzo Ignazio Thjulen, resident in Bologna, which were written between 1795 and 1797.

62 While all 45 pencil figures in the Bologna sketch-book are similar in appearance and style to those in the Paestum compositional drawings and plates (many wearing the distinctive hat and costume, apart from the hooded figures), not all appear to have been used. This tends to bears out the fact that, under these exceptional circumstances, Giovanni Battista had decided to accumulate a store of such characters for potential use, bearing in mind Francesco's inexperience. Elsewhere in the father's work, virtually none of the surviving figure studies, which number well over a hundred examples to date, can be related to a specific etched counterpart. For examples, see Thomas 1954, op. cit., pp.25–6; R. Bacou, 'A propos des dessins de figures de Piranèse' in *Piranèse et les Français*, ed. Brunel, 1978, op. cit., pp.33–42. While Professor Zamboni considers these figures to be the work of Francesco, Roberto Pane in his detailed study on the Paestum folio also attributes these figure studies (as well as one for grazing cows) to Giovanni Battista in terms of the sheer immediacy and confidence of the draughtsman-ship (*Paestum nelle Acqueforti di Piranesi*, 1980, op. cit., pp.125–6). However, in the case of the study of the watercarrier (FIG.41), Pane sees traces of Francesco's work in minor retouchings to his father's drawing (caption to Pane 1980, fig.89); similarly in the case of the squared study of a standing man with pipe which appears in the colonnade of Plate XIX (the compositional study for which is in the Rijksmuseum, FIG.18). Pane, incidentally, also suggests the hooded figures, such as those appearing in the studies for Plates III, XI and XVI (FIGS 20, 28 and 30 respectively) may have been shepherds affected by malaria, wearing protective clothing.

63 For example, the relative dimensions of the over-all height of the watercarrier in Plate XIII (FIG.35) are 116 mm in the Soane compositional drawing (FIG.34), 115 mm in the etched plate (FIG.42), but 172 mm in the squared outline drawing (FIG.41) in the Bologna sketchbook. In the case of the hooded figure at the centre of Plate XVI, the height is 87 mm in the Soane drawing (FIG.30, 44), 88 mm in the etched plate but 165mm in the squared sketch-book figure (FIG.43). (In Plate III a similar hooded figure standing in the colonnade, in reverse, may possibly have come from the same source.) To gain an idea of Francesco's etched figure style without such direct aid from his father, it is only necessary to examine the humanity populating his compositions which were based on the latter's Pompeian compositional studies in the volumes of his *Antiquités de la Grande Grèce* (1804–7).

64 For a sectional drawing by Soufflot of part of the crypt of Ste-Geneviève, c. 1758 (Archives Nationales, Paris), showing the Greek Doric columns in question, see A. Braham, *The Architecture of the French Enlightenment*, London, 1980, p.74, fig.90.

65 Chambers's dismissal of the Greek Doric in a draft for a Royal Academy lecture (RIBA Collection) is quoted in Pevsner and Lang 1968, op. cit., I, pp.205–06.

66 For the sketchbook containing Soane's reaction to the Doric temples on his second visit, entitled 'Italian Sketches/J. Soane/1779' (SM vol.39) and containing notes and measured sketches of antiq-uities, chiefly Pompeii and Paestum, see *Soane. Connoisseur & Collector*, 1995, op. cit., no.A5. See also P. de la Ruffinière Du Prey, *John Soane's Architectural Education: 1753–80*, London and New York, 1977, pp.184–5. On the left-hand page of the opening illustrated in FIG.45, Soane writes under the plan of the Temple of Juno (Athena): 'Going from Naples to Paestum by land this is the first Temple you arrive at'.

67 This watercolour by Soane's pupil C.J. Richardson, c. 1835 (SM 14/4/2), is based on his master's original design, dated *Romae, 1779*. The design seems to have been inspired by the Earl Bishop's comment to Soane, made when they were exploring the villa of Lucullus, near Terracina, that 'I should like to form some idea of a classical dog kennel, as I intend to build one at the Downhill [one of his Irish seats] for the hounds of my eldest son … This will be a fine subject for the display of your creative talents' (J. Soane, *Memoirs of the Professional Life of an Architect between the Years 1768 and 1835 Written by Himself*, privately printed, London, 1835, p.15). See Royal Academy, *Soane*, op. cit., p.107, no.26.

68 For Goethe's intellectual and artistic encounters with Paestum, see 'Goethe and Architecture' in N. Pevsner, *Studies in Art, Architecture and Design*, 1968, op. cit., I, p.169.

69 Quoted from Goethe, *Italian Journey [Italienische Reise]*, 1786–88, trans. by W.H. Auden and E. Mayer, London, 1970, p.218. See also another Goethe comment on Paestum in note 44 above.

70 In 1779, shortly after visiting Paestum, Soane sub-mitted this revised version of his *Triumphal Bridge* of 1776 (see note 4 above) for admission to the Academy of Parma, giving prominent use to the Greek Doric order. Twenty years later he reworked the design and got Gandy to produce this worm's-eye watercolour perspective (SM 12/5/6), exhibited at the Royal Academy in 1799. See *Soane. Connoisseur & Collector*, 1995, op. cit., no.38.

71 Watkin, *Soane. Academy Lectures*, p.526.

72 The design for a sepulchral church for the Duke of York, derived from a projected design for a family chapel at Tyringham (1800), and rendered here (FIG.49) in Gandy's watercolour perspective (SM P275) of 1827, involved three separate Paestum Doric porticoes.

73 Among lecture drawings based on Piranesi compositions is the *Entrance to a Roman building with an avenue of lions* (SM 20/8/14, repr. Watkin, *Soane. Academy Lectures*, pl.III) largely based on Piranesi's fantasy, *Ingresso d'un Antico Ginnasio*, added to the *Opere Varie* after 1757 (repr. Wilton-Ely, *Piranesi. Complete Etchings*, I, p.84, no.46). For Turner, whose perspective diagrams were derived from Piranesi's *Carcere Oscura* (Dark Prison) in the *Prima Parte*, see *Turner, 1775–1851*, exh. cat., Tate Gallery, London, 1974, p.181, nos B54 b and c, repr.

74 Watkin, *Soane. Academy Lectures*, Lecture VI, p. 603. Chambers's condemnation of Piranesi's

vast fantasy plan of an academy, *Pianta di Ampio Magnifico Collegio*, published in his *Opere Varie* in 1750 (Wilton-Ely, *Piranesi. Complete Etchings*, I, no.44) in the former's *Treatise on Civil Architecture* (1791 edition) was repeated by Soane in his Lecture XI (see Watkin, op. cit., p.647, fig.60).

75 H. Walpole, *Anecdotes of Painting*, London, 4th edition, 1780, IV, 'Advertisement', p.398.

76 The influence of Piranesi's archaeological plates involving multiple objects is discussed in S. Feinberg Millenson, *Sir John Soane's Museum*, UMI Research Press, Michigan, 1979, pp.97–8. For example the disproportionate scale between huge fragments and diminutive figures in the second frontispiece to *Le Antichità Romane*, Vol.II (FIG.7), is echoed in an early arrangement of the Dome area, looking east, recorded in a pen and watercolour view of the Dome area by lamplight, looking south-east, of 1811 by Joseph Gandy (SM 14/6/5), reproduced in Royal Academy, *Soane*, p.160, cat.68. Similarly, an early arrangement by Soane of a pile of miscellaneous fragments, topped by the Cawdor Vase, in the Dome area, as recorded in a watercolour of 1812 by George Basevi (SM 14/6/7), appears to have been directly inspired by a similar composition of unrelated marbles in Piranesi's plate of works from the Aufrere and Palmerston collections in his *Vasi, Candelabri, Cippi, Sarcofagi …*, 1778, I, Pl.49 (Wilton-Ely, *Piranesi. Complete Etchings*, II, no.934). For a summary of these observations, see S. Feinberg [Millenson], 'The genesis of Sir John Soane's Museum idea: 1801–1810', *Journal of the Society of Architectural Historians*, XLIII (October 1984), pp.225–37.

77 Soane's 'pasticcio' in the Monument Court at the very centre of the Museum was created in 1819 with truly Piranesian eclecticism to represent various styles of architecture. FIG.50 is an early record of it as it appeared in 1825 (SM vol.82/72); see P. Thornton and H. Dorey, *A Miscellany of Objects from Sir John Soane's Museum*, 1992, pp.30–31, fig.24. Soane described it as 'composed of the pedestal upon which the Cast of the Belvidere [sic] Apollo, now in the Museum, was charged; a marble Capital of Hindù Architecture; a Capital in stone, of the same dimensions and design as those of the Temple of Tivoli and another Capital in the Gothic gusto. These are surmounted by Architectural Groups of varied forms composed of fragments from different works, chiefly in cast iron, placed one upon the other, the whole terminated by a Pine-apple' (J. Soane, *Description*, 1835, p.29). By 1896 the *pasticcio* had become unstable and it was dismantled. Three large pieces survive and it will be reinstated as part of the restoration of the three courtyards at the Soane Museum in 2002–3.

In 1820 Mrs Soane's dog Fanny was buried in a similar column in the front courtyard. In 1824–5 this column was moved to the Monk's Yard, behind No.14, where it remains today. It is flanked in the yard by picturesque medieval ruins, salvaged during Soane's work at the Palace of Westminster. The complex history of the *pasticcio* is covered, with other contemporary illustrations, in H. Dorey, 'The Monk's Yard' in *Visions of Ruin. Architectural Fantasies & Designs for Garden Follies*, exh. cat., Sir John Soane's Museum, London, 1999, pp.51–2 and H. Dorey, 'Sir John Soane's Courtyard Gardens at Lincoln Inn Fields' in *The London Gardener*, the Journal of the London Historic parks and Gardens Trust, Volume 5, 1999–2000, pp.14–21.

78 Piranesi's highly evocative Roman Piazza de' Cavalieri di Malta, with its arcane monuments, which would have been exceptionally inspirational to the young Soane, is reproduced in detail in J. Wilton-Ely, 'Piranesi's symbolic images on the Aventine: the Piazza and Priory Church of the Knights of Malta, Rome', *Apollo*, CIII (March 1976), pp.214–27.

79 Gandy's aerial cut-away perspective of the entire Bank of England from the south-east, a Piranesian image on many levels, was exhibited at the Royal Academy in 1830 (no.1052) SM P267. See Royal Academy, *Soane*, op. cit., p.222, no.119).

80 The nature and implications of Soane's manuscript, *Crude Hints toward an History of my House*, together with a full transcription and notes, are provided in H. Dorey, 'Crude Hints' in *Visions of Ruin*, 1999, op. cit., pp.53–78. See also G. Darley, *John Soane*, New Haven and London, 1999, pp. 215, 299.

81 Joseph Gandy's awesome panorama, inscribed 'ARCHITECTURAL/Visions of early fancy/IN the gay morning of youth/And dreams in the even.g/of life' (SM P81), was exhibited at the Royal Academy in 1820 (no.894). A key to the projected and unrealised works depicted is given in Royal Academy, *Soane*, pp.280–81, no.211. For Gandy, as the supreme interpreter of Soane's Piranesian visions, see J. Summerson, 'The vision of J.M. Gandy', in *Heavenly Mansions and Other Essays on Architecture*, London, 1949, pp.111–34.

82 T. de Quincey, *Confessions of an English Opium Eater* [London, 1821], ed. A. Hayter, Harmondsworth, 1976, p.106.

Further reading

J. Mordaunt Crook, *The Greek Revival. Neo-Classical Attitudes in British Architecture, 1760–1870*, London, 1972.

Gillian Darley, *John Soane. An Accidental Romantic*, New Haven and London, 1999.

A.W. Lawrence and R.A. Tomlinson, *Greek Architecture*, Harmondsworth, 1983.

Michael McCarthy, 'Documents on the Greek Revival in Architecture', *Burlington Magazine*, CXIV (November 1972), pp.760–69.

Robin Middleton and David Watkin, *Neo-Classical and Nineteenth Century Architecture*, London, 1982.

Pierre de la Ruffinière Du Prey, *John Soane. The Making of an Architect*, Chicago and London, 1982.

S.F. Millenson, *Sir John Soane's Museum*, UMI Research Press, Michigan, 1979.

Roberto Pane, *Paestum nelle Acqueforti di Piranesi*, Milan, 1980.

G.B. Piranesi, *Observations on the letter of Monsieur Mariette with Opinions on Architecture, and a Preface to a New Treatise on the Introduction and Progress of the Fine arts in Europe in Ancient Times*. Introduction by John Wilton-Ely. Translation by Caroline Beamish and David Britt. Getty Research Institute, Los Angeles, 2002.

Margaret Richardson and MaryAnne Stevens (eds), *John Soane Architect. Master of Space and Light*, exh. cat., Royal Academy of Arts, London, 1999.

Andrew Robison, *Piranesi. Early Architectural Fantasies. A Catalogue Raisonné of the Etchings*, Chicago and London, 1986.

Jonathan Scott, *Piranesi*, London and New York, 1975.

Joselita Raspi Serra (ed.), *La Fortuna di Paestum e la Memoria Moderna del Dorico*, 2 vols, Florence, 1986.

— (ed.), *Paestum and the Doric Revival, 1750–1830*, Florence, 1986.

—(ed.), *Paestum. Idea e Immagine. Antologia di Testi Critici e di Immagini di Paestum, 1750–1836*, Modena, 1990.

John Soane, *Description of the House and Museum on the North Side of Lincoln's Inn Fields*, London, 1830 (revised 1832 and 1835–6).

Dorothy Stroud, *Sir John Soane, Architect*, London, 1984 (Revised, 1996).

John Summerson, 'The Vision of J.M. Gandy', in *Heavenly Mansions and Other Essays on Architecture*, London, 1949, pp.111–34.

—, *A New Description of Sir John Soane's Museum*, 10th edition, London, 2001.

Peter Thornton and Helen Dorey, *A Miscellany of Objects from Sir John Soane's Museum*, London, 1992.

Visions of Ruin. Architectural Fantasies & Designs for Garden Follies, with Crude Hints Towards a History of my House by John Soane, exh. cat., Sir John Soane's Museum, London, 1999.

Giles Waterfield (ed.), *Soane and Death. The Tombs and Monuments of Sir John Soane*, exh. cat., Dulwich Picture Gallery, 1996.

David Watkin, *Sir John Soane. Enlightenment Thought and the Royal Academy Lectures*, Cambridge, 1996.

Dora Wiebenson, *Sources of Greek Revival Architecture*, London, 1969.

John Wilton-Ely (ed.), *Piranesi. The Polemical Works*, Farnborough, 1972.

—, *The Mind and Art of Piranesi*, London and New York, 1978.

—, *Piranesi as Architect and Designer*, New Haven and London, 1993.

—, *Giovanni Battista Piranesi: The Complete Etchings*, 2 vols, San Francisco, 1994.

G.B. Piranesi's own publications

1743	*Prima Parte di Architetture e Prospettive*
c. 1745	*Grotteschi; Invenzioni capric di Carceri*
1745	Plates published by Fausto Amidei in *Varie Vedute di Roma Antica e Moderna* (several of them being of a earlier date)
c. 1748 (or earlier)–1778	*Vedute di Roma*
1748	*Antichità Romane de' Tempi della Repubblica e de' Primi Imperatori*
c. 1750	*Opere Varie di Architettura, Prospettiva, Grotteschi Antichità* (reprint of Prima Parte, except for one plate, with additions, plus the *Grotteschi*)
1750	*Camere Sepolcrali degli Antichi romani le quali estistono dentro e di fuori di Roma*
1751	*Le Magnificenze di Roma* (composite publication by Giovanni Bouchard containing a selection of the early plates of the *Vedute di Roma*)
1753	*I Trofei di Ottaviano Augusto*
1756	*Le Antichità Romane*
1757	*Lettere di Giustificazione scritte a Milord Charlemont*
c. 1760	*Carceri d'Invenzione* (reworking of *Invenzioni capric di Carceri* with two additional plates)
1761	*Della Magnificenza ed Architettura de' Romani; Catologo della Opere* (subsequently revised in many states); *Le Rovine del Castello dell'Acqua Giulia*
1762	*Lapides Capitolini; Descrizione e Disegno dell' Emissario del Lago Albano; Di due Spelonche ornate dagli Antichi alla Riva del Lago Albano; Il Campo Marzio dell'Antica Roma;*
1764	*Antichità di Albano e di Castelgandolfo; Antichità di Cora; Raccolta di Alcuni Disegni del … Guercino*
1765	*Osservazioni sopra la lettre de M.Mariette*, accompanied by *Parere su l'Architettura* and *Della Introduzione e del Progresso delle belle arti in Europa de' tempi antichi*
after 1765	*Alcune Vedute di Archi Trionfali* (reprint of *Antichità Romane de' Tempi della Repubblica e de' Primi Imperatori*
1769	*Diverse Maniere d'adornare i Cammini*
1774–9	*Trofeo o sia Magnifica Colonna Coclide*
c. 1774	*Pianta di Roma e del Campo Marzio*
1778	*Vasi, Candelabri, Cippi, Sarcofagi …; Différentes vues de trois grands édifices qui subsistent encore nel milieu de l'ancienne ville de Pesto*

Posthumous publications issued by Francesco Piranesi

1781	*Pianta delle fabbriche esistenti nella Villa Adriana*
1791	*Dimostrazione dell'Emissario del Lago Fucino*
1804–7	*Les antiquités de la Grande Grèce*

Concordance of drawings and etchings

This concordance identifies the drawings by Giovanni Battista Piranesi in Sir John Soane's Museum that were published in *Différentes vues de trois grands édifices qui subsistent encore dans le milieu de l'ancienne ville de Pesto* (1778)

Figure	Soane no.	Piranesi etchings
FIG.19	SM P71	Plate II
FIG.20	SM P51	Plate III
FIG.21	SM P146	Plate IV
FIG.22	SM P76	Plate V
FIG.23	SM P75	Plate VI
FIG.24	SM P133	Plate VIII
FIG.25	SM P54	Plate VII
FIG.26	SM P125	Plate IX
FIG.27	SM P72	Plate X
FIG.28	SM P70	Plate XI
FIG.29	SM P69	Plate XII
FIG.30	SM P139	Plate XVI
FIG.31	SM P77	Plate XIV
FIG.32	SM P140	Plate XVII
FIG.33	SM P140	Plate XVII
FIG.34	SM P74	Plate XIII

Photo credits

Cover, FIGS 1–11, 12, 14, 15, 19–37, 39, 42, 44–46, 48–54 Sir John Soane's Museum

FIG.13   In the collection of The Duke of Buccleuch & Queensbury, KT

FIG.14   The British Library

FIGS 16, 22, 38   ©The British Museum

FIG.17   Cliché Bibliothèque Nationale de France, Paris

FIG.18   Rijksmuseum, Amsterdam

Fig.40   Staatliche Museen zu Berlin, Kunstbibliothek, Berlin

FIGS 41, 43   Biblioteca Estense, Modena

FIG.47   photo © Ptolemy Dean

Frontispiece   Museo di Roma